FALAFEL
FOR BREAKFAST

TO OUR PARENTS, WHO TAUGHT US
THE VALUE OF FAMILY, SHARING AND,
OF COURSE, GOOD FOOD.

MICHAEL RANTISSI
& KRISTY FRAWLEY

FALAFEL
FOR BREAKFAST

MODERN MIDDLE EASTERN RECIPES
FOR ANY TIME OF THE DAY FROM
KEPOS STREET KITCHEN

MURDOCH BOOKS

FOREWORD

MICHAEL ARRIVED IN SYDNEY IN 2005, COMING FROM TEL AVIV AND HAVING WORKED AT SOME OF THE MOST CELEBRATED RESTAURANTS AROUND THE WORLD. HE WORKED AS A SOUS CHEF IN THE FINE-DINING KITCHEN AT THE BATHERS' PAVILION RESTAURANT, A ROLE HE HELD FOR OVER THREE YEARS.

Michael has an inquisitive mind and is always on a path to discovery. With great skills and a creative talent, he also possesses the physical robustness to face the pressure and long work hours in the kitchen. As with any talented chef, I knew the time would come for him to lead his own kitchen and, when the opportunity came, I could only give my blessing.

Michael always stayed in touch with me and the Bathers' team, and to my great joy my extremely hardworking personal assistant and office manager, Kristy Frawley, became his partner. This pairing was only going to lead to great things.

It did not take long for Michael and Kristy to spot a run-down restaurant in the inner Sydney suburb of Redfern. Kepos Street Kitchen was on the way. Their hard work revamping the place made it a more airy, casual space to take advantage of its somewhat bohemian location.

Kristy, with her infinite drive and experience, set herself to creating systems, dealing with building applications, organising a logo and branding, developing a business plan and promoting the new bistro and Michael's food. Initially she even had the task of baking the cakes for the bistro while at the same time working at The Bathers' Pavilion. This left Michael free to renovate the space, ready his kitchen and design the menus for what was to come in this great little neighbourhood eatery.

It felt only natural for Michael to gravitate to the food of his childhood – dishes he loved that are deeply rooted in his food memories. The mixture of Mediterranean dishes influenced by Middle Eastern and Israeli favourites runs true to his aspirations and heritage.

Kepos Street Kitchen opened in 2012, serving bistro food with a modern approach based on the cuisine of the Middle East. Dishes such as falafel, kibbeh and hummus are served with a modern twist, and ingredients including pomegranate, dates, burghul and labneh feature on the menu over breakfast, lunch and dinner. Never have these ingredients been fresher or more delicious.

I cannot recall such an immediate success. It was helped by the recognition of the Sydney food press that Michael and Kristy deserved to be acknowledged as pioneers in this style of cuisine, and that they recognised Michael's natural talent. Kepos Street Kitchen became a new favourite food destination for Sydneysiders, and deservingly so.

Now we have Michael's recipes in a beautiful cookbook, so people can find inspiration and joy from what I think is some of the most delicious food I have eaten in Australia.

Serge Dansereau
Chef & Owner, The Bathers' Pavilion, Sydney

CONTENTS

INTRODUCTION

SERENDIPITY IS A WORD THAT'S NEW TO ME – I CAN'T QUITE THINK OF ITS EQUIVALENT IN MY NATIVE TONGUE – BUT I LEARNT IT THANKS TO MY OWN MOMENT OF, WELL, SERENDIPITY, SO IT'S ONE I WILL ALWAYS LOVE.

It all started when Kristy (my partner) and I were on the way to the shops and passed the near-derelict site of a once-popular inner-city café. With Kristy's profession firmly in the hospitality industry for 20 years, and me being a chef for almost as long, we were casually discussing how nice it would be to have a place of our own – maybe even that place. On our return trip 20 minutes later, lugging bags full of groceries, we noticed a 'For Lease' sign on the side of the building.

The following weeks – exciting, crazy, daunting and exhilarating – were spent transforming my life as head chef in someone else's business to owner-operator of my own. Luckily, all our dear friends and family members put up their hands to help, and it seemed we knew someone with just about every skill and talent needed to get a restaurant up and running.

We started work and hung out a sign announcing our vision. It said, 'Once the makeover is complete we'll be creating breakfast, lunch and dinner menus filled with the fresh, the fabulous and the favourite, all with a Middle Eastern accent. It's food we hope will excite and thrill you, and make you say our favourite words: "Oh yum! Oh wow! That's the most delicious thing I've ever eaten!"'

A big promise, yes, but we were full of enthusiasm and optimism.

Soon, the wreck we'd adopted emerged looking light, bright and hopeful. Two months later Kepos Street

Kitchen was officially open, and the word serendipity – unexpected pleasure and surprising good fortune or, as I like to think of it, being in the right place at exactly the right time – became part of my vocabulary.

Writing the menus for our little café was liberating because for the first time I could cook the food I wanted to cook, rather than having to adhere to the philosophy of the restaurant owner for whom I was working.

The starting points for every dish were the flavours and ingredients of my childhood in Israel, and recipes learnt by watching my mum work her way around the kitchen and then presenting the dishes to my dad, brothers, sisters and me. Next came the influences of the classic cooking techniques I'd mastered during my time studying in New York and years working in fine-dining restaurants in Paris, Tokyo, London, Tel Aviv and, of course, my new home of Sydney.

Those first menus, and every one since, are a culinary autobiography of sorts – a collection of dishes that I love to eat and cook, and, more importantly, the food that receives the most applause from my family and friends when I am cooking at home.

Kristy and I were shocked and humbled when customers started queuing to eat in our tiny restaurant. You couldn't wipe the smile (or the disbelief) off my face. Our most-cherished regulars are the good people of the inner city, but we also have wonderful supporters from

farther afield. It seems the Middle Eastern flavours that are so familiar and delicious to me, are what surprise and delight our customers; the food that makes me happy, makes others happy, too.

Soon, a little more serendipity came to pass. At the same time our small patch in Redfern was gaining popularity, cooks and food-lovers beyond started to find inspiration in Middle Eastern flavours. A new culinary vocabulary was being learnt. The generosity and spirit of shared dishes, as we eat in my homeland, was being embraced in restaurants and homes around Australia. The essential spices of the Middle East – such as cumin, sumac, cinnamon and saffron – and the versatile aromatic mixes for which they are the foundation – like za'atar, baharat, dukkah and chermoula – were appearing more often in kitchens around the country.

People were filling their shopping trolleys with couscous, chickpeas, dates, pistachios, almonds, lemons, pomegranates, mint, coriander and pita bread. Dishes like shakshuka, kibbeh neah and bourekas were catching up with the familiar hummus, tabouleh and falafel of the local kebab shop.

Vegetables were also moving from side dish to star of the show. The usual Aussie favourites – like tomato, cucumber, eggplant (aubergine), zucchini (courgette), beetroot (beets) and cauliflower, and other seasonal offerings from the Mediterranean vegie patch – were being approached with Middle Eastern dishes in mind. People were making plate upon plate of healthful, flavourful and joyful salads, so wonderful they could convert even the most devout carnivore into a committed vegetarian – well, a part-time one, at least.

The timing was right for a cookbook. So the ingredient lists, measurements and methods that lived in my head were soon being scribbled onto bits of paper mid-service, and then handed to Kristy to decipher and shape into recipes that would enable you to create these dishes in your home.

The book begins the way every day should: with breakfast. Specifically, *Falafel for Breakfast*. A curious title, I know, for a book that also takes in lunch and dinner, and the joys of small snacks and celebratory meals, but a title with a story. It reflects my mum's incredulity that bacon-and-egg and toast-and-Vegemite-loving Aussies were coming to Kepos first thing in the morning and ordering falafel. Equally, no one in my family ever would have dreamed that 'Dad's favourite brekkie' – a selection of hummus, tomato, boiled egg and the ubiquitous falafel of my childhood – would be one of the most popular items on the menu.

In giving you this collection of recipes, I'm hoping to begin the chain of sharing that is at the heart of a great Middle Eastern feast. Start by creating your own menu: finding the mix that suits the day, the season, the occasion, the mood. Then, gather your friends and family to the table, and watch how the food you've made starts conversations that will define the moment. The more dishes, the more the chatter as people pass a dish here, and comment on it there. It's the way I always remember mealtimes when I was growing up and how I like my food to be enjoyed now.

Don't let recipes intimidate you. Kristy's approach is, I think, perfect. She is always happy to change a recipe to suit her needs, and the result will often be delicious. She reminds me that the best cooking is purely about using your instincts and the ingredients at hand.

I started working in restaurant kitchens in Tel Aviv for pocket money. I certainly never thought then I would become a chef owning a modern Middle Eastern restaurant in Sydney and writing a cookbook about it. But I am ecstatic about sharing these recipes and this way of eating with you.

Michael Rantissi

CHAPTER ONE

BREAKFAST & BRUNCH

IN THE MIDDLE EAST, WE TAKE OUR BREAKFASTS VERY SERIOUSLY.

We think of it as the most important meal of the day, and the classic approach is to serve a collection of dishes for people to share. You'll find food to suit all tastes here, from egg and bacon rolls and chocolate granola to shakshuka and tea-soaked eggs. At Kepos Street Kitchen, we have incorporated some Middle Eastern breakfast staples in a menu item we call 'Dad's favourite brekkie' (see page 24). And as the title of the book suggests, no breakfast is complete without falafel.

It takes time to make good falafel so you'll need to start this recipe 24 hours in advance. To shape the falafel you can use a traditional falafel spoon, available at most Middle Eastern grocery stores. Alternatively, you can use two tablespoons, or do it the Egyptian way and make small patties with your hands. (If using either of the latter shaping methods, adding 2 egg whites when seasoning the mixture will make it firmer – although, because it is not traditional, I prefer not to add egg whites.)

FALAFEL

MAKES 20

200 g (7 oz/1 cup) dried chickpeas
100 g (3½ oz) dried split
    broad beans
1 large handful coriander (cilantro),
    leaves picked
2 large handfuls flat-leaf (Italian)
    parsley, leaves picked
1 small onion, coarsely chopped
2 long red chillies, seeds removed,
    finely chopped
4 garlic cloves, coarsely chopped
1 teaspoon baking powder
1 teaspoon ground cumin
2 tablespoons sesame seeds
rice bran oil, for deep-frying

In a large bowl, soak the chickpeas and broad beans overnight in cold water, changing the water at least twice during this time.

Drain the chickpeas and broad beans and put them in a food processor with the coriander, parsley, onion, chilli and garlic. Whiz until grainy (not a smooth purée).

Transfer the mixture to a bowl and add the baking powder, cumin and sesame seeds. Mix together and, using a falafel spoon or two tablespoons, quenelle the mixture or roll it by hand into 20 patties.

Pour enough rice bran oil for deep-frying into a large deep saucepan and heat to 170°C (325°F). To test if the oil is hot enough, drop in a cube of bread and if it turns golden brown in 20 seconds you are good to start cooking. (If the oil is not hot enough, the falafel will break up.)

Working in batches, drop the falafel into the oil and deep-fry for 3 minutes, or until golden. Remove the falafel with a slotted spoon and drain on paper towel. Serve with green tahini (pictured right, see page 205) or hummus (see page 210).

A beautiful start to the day, providing everything your body needs, including vegies and protein. Make this tasty dish on weekends when you have extra time to cook and enjoy eating it.

ZUCCHINI FRITTERS WITH SMOKED SALMON & POACHED EGGS

MAKES 8 LARGE FRITTERS (SERVES 4)

300 g (10½ oz) zucchini (courgettes), coarsely grated
1 teaspoon table salt
1 small onion, finely diced
2 garlic cloves, finely diced
1 large handful flat-leaf (Italian) parsley, leaves chopped
1 handful mint, leaves chopped
1 handful dill, chopped, reserving some sprigs for garnish
2 eggs, plus 8 eggs extra, to poach
40 g (1½ oz) wholemeal (whole-wheat) plain (all-purpose) or plain (all-purpose) flour, sifted
50 g (1¾ oz) goat's cheese, broken into chunks
50 g (1¾ oz) ricotta cheese
2 tablespoons olive oil
8 large slices smoked salmon, to serve

Put the grated zucchini in a bowl and sprinkle with the salt. Mix well and leave for 30 minutes, then strain the excess liquid off and discard. Place the zucchini in a large bowl.

Add the onion, garlic, parsley, mint, dill and 2 eggs to the zucchini and mix well. Add the flour and mix to combine. Fold in the goat's cheese and ricotta cheese without overmixing – it is nice to have big chunks in the mixture.

Heat the olive oil in a non-stick frying pan over medium heat. Spoon ¼ cup of the mixture into the pan and cook for 2 minutes, or until golden brown, then flip and cook the other side (see note below).

Poach the 8 eggs so the yolks are still runny, or to your liking.

Serve the fritters layered with smoked salmon and topped with the poached eggs. Garnish with the dill sprigs.

NOTE
If you like your fritters crispier, put them in a preheated 180°C (350°F) oven for an extra 5 minutes after frying.

You will need to eat these eggs on the day they are prepared, either warm or at room temperature. Serve sliced with bourekas (see page 42) or as a dish at a shared breakfast table.

TEA-SOAKED EGGS

MAKES 10

7 English Breakfast teabags
10 eggs

Pour 2 litres (70 fl oz/8 cups) water into a large saucepan, add the teabags and bring to the boil. Once the water is boiling, turn off the heat and cool the water to room temperature.

Carefully add the eggs to the room-temperature water and bring back to boiling point. Boil the eggs for 5 minutes. Turn off the heat.

Take out an egg and roll it on a work surface so the shell starts to crackle – this will allow the tea water to seep into the egg, giving it a lovely tan colour and a crackled appearance. Repeat with all of the eggs, returning them to the hot tea water (with the heat turned off) for 5 minutes to steep.

Peel the eggs and put them back into the water until ready to serve.

Great served with toasted sourdough or on its own for breakfast, you could also eat this spiced egg salad with smoked salmon, basturma or salami on the side.

SPICED EGG SALAD

SERVES 4

8 eggs
½ teaspoon coriander seeds
½ teaspoon cumin seeds
3–4 spring onions (scallions), green and white parts chopped
1 handful coriander (cilantro), leaves finely chopped
4 tablespoons good-quality mayonnaise
¼ teaspoon ground turmeric

Boil the eggs for 5–6 minutes.

Meanwhile, toast the coriander and cumin seeds in a dry frying pan over medium heat until aromatic. Lightly crush the seeds using a mortar and pestle.

Peel and either coarsely grate or roughly chop the eggs (the white will be firm but the yolks will still be soft and slightly oozing). Put in a medium bowl, add the remaining ingredients and gently mix to combine. Season with salt and freshly ground black pepper to taste.

Be as creative as you like with this recipe – you can use any type or combination of seeds, or leave them out and use puffed quinoa as a topping. Or you can simply serve the yoghurt with the strawberries and pomegranate.

MIXED BERRY & POMEGRANATE YOGHURT WITH TOASTED SEEDS

SERVES 4–6

1 kg (2 lb 4 oz) plain yoghurt (see page 231 for our homemade yoghurt recipe)

500 g (1 lb 2 oz) mixed berries (such as strawberries and blackberries), washed, hulled and cut in half if desired

1 pomegranate, seeded (keep the seeds) and juiced (keep to make pomegranate molasses or drinks)

3 tablespoons pomegranate molasses (see page 229)

1 tablespoon honey

50 g (1¾ oz) pepitas (pumpkin seeds), toasted

50 g (1¾ oz) sunflower seeds, toasted

50 g (1¾ oz) whole almonds, skin on, toasted and chopped

50 g (1¾ oz) pistachio nut kernels

Divide the yoghurt between four to six serving bowls. Top with the berries and pomegranate seeds.

Mix together the pomegranate molasses and honey. Drizzle over the yoghurt and berries.

Combine the pepitas, sunflower seeds, almonds and pistachio nut kernels, and scatter over each serve.

The delicious egg and bacon rolls we serve at Kepos Street Kitchen need not so much a recipe, but instructions on how to puzzle together a set of wonderful ingredients.

EGG & BACON ROLLS

MAKES 4

2 roma (plum) or truss tomatoes
olive oil, to drizzle
1 handful thyme, leaves picked
4 large brioche buns, cut in half
    and toasted
4 tablespoons chilli jam
    (see page 221)
8 tablespoons aïoli
    (see page 226)
100 g (3½ oz) baby spinach, wilted
8 slices of crispy cooked bacon
8 eggs, fried as desired

To roast the tomatoes, preheat the oven to 200°C (400°F). Cut each tomato lengthways into quarters and put on a baking tray lined with baking paper. Drizzle the tomatoes with olive oil and sprinkle with sea salt, freshly ground black pepper and the thyme leaves. Roast for 20 minutes.

To assemble the egg and bacon rolls, spread the cut halves of the toasted brioche buns with the chilli jam and aïoli. On the bottom half of each brioche roll, place some tomatoes, wilted spinach and bacon. Top with 2 fried eggs and the other half of the brioche roll and serve immediately.

A take on another dish my mum made with potato chips and sausages for my brothers, sisters and me when we were kids, this is topped with basturma – a seasoned air-dried and cured beef available from Middle Eastern grocery stores. You can prepare the polenta a day ahead, as it needs at least 3 hours to set in the fridge.

FETA SCRAMBLED EGGS WITH POLENTA CHIPS & BASTURMA

SERVES 4

1 quantity polenta (see page 236)
vegetable or rice bran oil, for
    deep-frying
50 g (1¾ oz/¼ cup) polenta,
    for dusting
50 g (1¾ oz/⅓ cup) plain
    (all-purpose) flour, for dusting
100 g (3½ oz/⅔ cup) crumbled
    good-quality Greek feta
2 handfuls flat-leaf (Italian) parsley,
    leaves chopped
½ teaspoon dried mint
8 eggs
2½ tablespoons thin (pouring)
    cream (or use milk)
3 tablespoons olive oil, for frying,
    plus extra, to drizzle
16 thin slices basturma or similar
    air-dried beef product

Make the tray of polenta a day ahead. Cut into finger-sized (1 cm x 1 cm x 4 cm/½ inch x ½ inch x 1½ inch) batons.

Pour enough vegetable or rice bran oil into a frying pan to deep-fry the polenta batons. Heat to 170°C (325°F) or when a cube of bread dropped into the oil turns golden brown in 20 seconds.

In a medium bowl, combine the polenta and flour. Add the polenta batons and gently dust with the flour mixture.

Shake off the excess flour mixture and fry the batons in the hot oil in batches for 1–2 minutes, or until golden. Drain on paper towel.

Put the feta, parsley and mint in a bowl. Toss gently to combine and set aside.

Put the eggs and cream in a bowl and whisk to combine.

Heat the olive oil in a frying pan over high heat and pour in the egg mixture. Turn the heat off (do not overcook the eggs as they should be nice and soft) and gently move or scramble the eggs around the pan using a plastic spatula. Scatter over the feta and herb mixture and gently scramble through.

To serve, place a large spoonful of scrambled eggs on each plate with a few polenta batons. Top with the basturma and a drizzle of olive oil.

DAD'S FAVOURITE BREKKIE

Bringing together a number of our signature dishes (including falafel, of course), this combination is a classic breakfast back home, and one my father likes very much. Serve the recipes shown here with boiled eggs, vine-ripened tomatoes, fresh mint leaves, sea salt and toasted grainy bread.

1 **FALAFEL** see page 14
2 **HAZELNUT DUKKAH** see page 212
3 **HUMMUS** see page 210
4 **LABNEH** see page 209
5 **MINT & LEMON TEA** see page 199

Originating in North Africa, shakshuka has become a traditional Israeli dish that every family makes – and that every family makes differently. I make my version quite spicy with more paprika and cumin coming through, but if you'd like it lighter you can reduce or omit some of the spices. You can also add greens to this dish – spinach works really well. This is a very satisfying and easy dish to make, and it can be served straight from the pan. You can make the sauce in advance, too, and reheat it when you start cooking the eggs.

SHAKSHUKA

SERVES 4

4 tablespoons olive oil
1 small brown onion, diced
5 garlic cloves, diced
2 large green chillies,
    diced (optional)
2 large red capsicums (peppers),
    coarsely diced
1 tablespoon mild paprika
1 tablespoon ground coriander
1 tablespoon ground cumin
2 tablespoons tomato paste
    (concentrated purée)
1 kg (2 lb 4 oz) ripe tomatoes,
    blanched and peeled (see note)
    and coarsely chopped
1 handful coriander (cilantro),
    leaves and stalks chopped
8 eggs
flat-leaf (Italian) parsley
    sprigs, to garnish
extra virgin olive oil, to drizzle

Heat the olive oil in a large ovenproof frying pan over medium heat. Add the onion and garlic and cook for 5 minutes. Add the chilli and capsicum and cook for 2 minutes. Add the paprika, ground coriander and cumin and cook for 2 minutes. Add the tomato paste and cook for 1 minute. Add the tomato and cook for 20 minutes, or until the sauce has reduced to the consistency of a tomato passata (puréed tomatoes). Season with salt and stir through the fresh coriander.

Gently crack the eggs over the tomato sauce in the pan, spacing them out, and cover with a lid. Reduce the heat to low and cook for 3 minutes, or until the egg whites start to cook. Remove the lid, increase the heat to medium and cook for a further 3–5 minutes, until the yolks are still runny but the whites are firm. Don't worry if the eggs are not fully cooked, as the heat of the sauce will continue to cook them. Remove from the heat. Scatter over the parsley sprigs, drizzle with extra virgin olive oil, season with salt and freshly ground black pepper, and serve.

NOTE
To blanch and peel the tomatoes, score a shallow cross in the base. Put in a heatproof bowl and cover with boiling water. Leave for 30 seconds, then transfer to cold water and peel away the skin from the cross.

I'm not sure of the official history of rice pudding but it has always been a part of mine since childhood. Here I have changed the traditional recipe and added almonds for crunch. I love serving rice pudding with a compote of stewed fruit – my favourite is dates stewed in pomegranate molasses (see page 229) for a nice sweet and sour flavour combination.

RICE PUDDING

SERVES 8-10

200 g (7 oz) short-grain white rice
1 litre (35 fl oz/4 cups) full-cream (whole) milk
200 g (7 oz/1¼ oz) blanched almonds, coarsely chopped
110 g (3¾ oz/½ cup) caster (superfine) sugar
200 ml (7 fl oz) thin (pouring) cream
200 ml (7 fl oz) full-cream (whole) milk, extra, chilled
stewed fruit and chopped nuts of your choice, to serve

Heat the rice and 700 ml (24 fl oz) water in a large saucepan over medium–high heat until almost boiling. Reduce the heat to low, cover with a lid and cook for 10 minutes. Increase the heat to medium, add 1 litre of milk and cook, stirring constantly, for 15 minutes.

Add the almonds and sugar and cook for 5 minutes. Remove from the heat and add the cream and extra cold milk. Serve warm or cold, topped with stewed fruit and sprinkled with chopped nuts.

My mum uses pumpkin, but sweet potato works just as well for these doughnuts, which are great to serve for brunch either as a sweet dish with a chocolate or caramel sauce, or as a savoury dish with a tzatziki dip (just reduce the sugar in the doughnuts to 1 tablespoon).

PUMPKIN DOUGHNUTS

MAKES ABOUT 20 MINI DOUGHNUTS

375 g (13 oz/2½ cups) peeled and chopped pumpkin or 250 g (9 oz/1 cup) readymade pumpkin purée
150 g (5½ oz/1 cup) plain (all-purpose) flour, sifted
2 tablespoons caster (superfine) sugar
2 teaspoons baking powder
1 egg, beaten
3 tablespoons full-cream (whole) milk
rice bran or vegetable oil, for frying

To make the pumpkin purée, preheat the oven to 180°C (350°F) and put the pumpkin pieces on a baking tray lined with baking paper. Cook for 40–45 minutes, until soft. Transfer to a bowl, allow to cool, then mash.

In a large bowl, combine the pumpkin purée, flour, sugar, baking powder, egg, milk and a pinch of salt.

Using a deep-fryer or a large deep saucepan, add the rice bran oil and heat to 170°C (325°F). If you don't have a thermometer, drop in a cube of bread – the oil is hot enough when the bread turns golden brown in 20 seconds.

Using 2 tablespoons, shape the mixture into rough balls and drop into the hot oil, a few at a time. Cook for 3–4 minutes, moving them around in the oil.

Drain on paper towel and repeat until all of the batter has been used. Serve immediately.

Tucking into a batch of pancakes on a Sunday morning will always bring out your inner child. Evan is the Kepos Street chef who created this recipe, where the flavours of the fluffy buttermilk pancakes are complemented by the pistachio praline, saffron crème pâtissière and silan (Israeli date 'honey') for a wonderfully indulgent breakfast. The batter can be made up to a day ahead and kept in the fridge.

EVAN'S DATE & BUTTERMILK PANCAKES WITH PISTACHIO PRALINE

SERVES 4

2 eggs, separated
375 ml (13 fl oz/1½ cups) buttermilk
2 tablespoons butter, melted
½ vanilla bean, halved lengthways
    and seeds scraped
225 g (8 oz/1½ cups)
    self-raising flour
1 teaspoon ground cinnamon
pinch of sea salt
1 tablespoon caster
    (superfine) sugar
150 g (5½ oz) Medjool dates,
    seeded and diced
oil spray for cooking
saffron crème pâtissière
    (see page 230), to serve
silan (Israeli date 'honey',
    see page 224), to serve
icing (confectioners') sugar,
    for dusting

PISTACHIO PRALINE
100 g (3½ oz) caster
    (superfine) sugar
100 g (3½ oz/¾ cup)
    pistachio nut kernels

To make the pistachio praline, line a baking tray with baking paper. Put the sugar and 25 ml (¾ fl oz) water in a saucepan over medium heat and stir with a wooden spoon until dissolved. Brush any crystals down from the side of the pan with a pastry brush dipped in cold water. Cook the syrup, without stirring, until it starts to colour. Continue cooking, swirling the pan gently, until golden. Tip in the nuts and stir to coat with a wooden spoon. Pour the mixture onto the prepared tray and spread evenly with a wooden spoon. Allow to cool completely.

To make the pancakes, whisk the egg yolks lightly in a jug. Add the buttermilk, melted butter and vanilla seeds, whisking until combined.

Sift the flour, cinnamon and salt into a medium bowl. Stir in the sugar. Make a well in the centre and add the egg yolk mixture, mixing lightly until smooth. Fold through the dates.

Whisk the egg whites until soft peaks form. Fold half of the egg white into the batter, being careful not to knock out the air. Repeat with the remaining egg white.

Heat a non-stick frying pan over low heat. Spray with cooking oil. Pour about ¾ cup of batter into the pan and cook for 2–3 minutes, until golden brown, then flip and cook the other side. Repeat with the remaining mixture, keeping the cooked pancakes warm.

Break up the praline and crush using a mortar and pestle or pulse in a food processor. Scatter the praline crumble over the pancakes and serve with a scoop of saffron crème pâtissière, a drizzle of silan and a dusting of icing sugar.

If you need to feed a crowd for breakfast, brunch or even lunch, cook up this tasty frittata. A great way to serve it is with a salad of spring onions, dill and parsley seasoned with lemon juice and olive oil on top.

LEEK & HERB FRITTATA

SERVES 4-6

3 tablespoons olive oil, plus extra for cooking the frittata
1 large leek, white part and half of the green part, sliced
2 teaspoons ground turmeric
10 eggs
3–4 spring onions (scallions), green and white parts finely chopped
1 handful dill, finely chopped
1 handful flat-leaf (Italian) parsley, finely chopped
4 kipfler (fingerling) potatoes, boiled, peeled and broken into large chunks

Preheat the oven to 180°C (350°F).

Heat the olive oil in a 24 cm (9½ in) non-stick ovenproof frying pan over medium heat. Add the leek and turmeric and cook for 2–3 minutes, just until the leek starts to steam. Transfer the leek to a large bowl, keeping the pan for the next step.

Add the eggs, spring onion, dill, parsley and potato to the leek mixture in the bowl. Mix well and season with salt and freshly ground black pepper to taste.

Return the frying pan to medium heat, adding more olive oil if necessary. Pour in the egg mixture and allow to cook for 1 minute. Transfer the pan to the oven and cook for 15–20 minutes, until the egg is cooked to your liking.

Flip the frittata onto a large plate to serve.

What is nice about this dish is you get chocolate milk and delicious granola in one bowl!

CHOCOLATE GRANOLA WITH BANANA & CARDAMOM MILK

MAKES 8-10 SERVES

50 ml (2½ tablespoons) vegetable oil or very light olive oil

4 tablespoons maple syrup

125 g (4½ oz/⅔ cup, lightly packed) dark brown sugar

1 vanilla bean, split lengthways and seeds scraped out

350 g (12 oz/3½ cups) rolled (porridge) oats

155 g (5½ oz/1 cup) chopped almonds

100 g (3½ oz/¾ cup) pistachio nut kernels

20 g (¾ oz/¼ cup) shredded coconut

40 g (1½ oz/⅓ cup) unsweetened cocoa powder

250 g (9 oz/1⅔ cups) good-quality dark chocolate melts (buttons)

½ teaspoon sea salt flakes

banana, to serve

CARDAMOM MILK

1 litre (35 fl oz/4 cups) full-cream (whole) milk

½ teaspoon ground cardamom

Preheat the oven to 140°C (275°F). Line a baking tray with baking paper.

Put the vegetable oil, maple syrup, sugar and vanilla seeds in a medium saucepan over medium–high heat and bring to the boil. Remove from the heat when just starting to boil and set aside.

Put the oats, almonds, pistachios, coconut and cocoa powder in a large bowl and mix well. Pour the melted sugar mixture over the dry ingredients and mix well with a metal spoon.

Spread the oat mixture out onto the prepared tray, transfer to the oven and cook for 30 minutes, or until the nuts and oats are golden brown, stirring every 10 minutes.

Remove the toasted oat mixture from the oven and transfer to a separate cold tray, to prevent further cooking. Allow to cool for 5 minutes.

Sprinkle the chocolate melts and sea salt over the oat mixture and put the tray into the fridge for 5 minutes, or until the chocolate is hard. Break the mixture into chunks with your hands and store in an airtight container for up to 3 weeks.

Make the cardamom milk when you are ready to serve the granola. Pour the milk into a medium saucepan and heat over medium–low heat until warm. Add the cardamom and whisk until the milk starts to froth, then remove from the heat and transfer the milk to a jug.

Serve the granola in individual bowls, with the cardamom milk and banana on the side for people to have as much as they like.

An easy dish because each of the elements can be prepared in advance and assembled trifle-style when you're ready for breakfast or brunch.

BREAKFAST COUSCOUS TRIFLE

SERVES 4

190 g (6¾ oz/1 cup) couscous
3 tablespoons light olive oil
½ teaspoon ground cinnamon
375 ml (13 fl oz/1½ cups)
    boiling water
200 g (7 oz) mixed berries (fresh
    or frozen)
½ teaspoon vanilla bean paste
1 cinnamon stick
½ teaspoon rosewater
80 g (2¾ oz) sugar
500 g (1 lb 2 oz) Greek-style yoghurt
3 tablespoons icing
    (confectioners') sugar
100 g (3½ oz) Turkish delight,
    coarsely chopped
1 pinch of saffron threads

Put the couscous, olive oil and ground cinnamon in a stainless steel bowl and mix well. Pour over the boiling water and cover the bowl tightly with plastic wrap. Set aside for 10–15 minutes.

Put the berries, vanilla bean paste, cinnamon stick, rosewater and sugar in a medium saucepan over medium–low heat and bring to a simmer. Cook for 15 minutes. Remove from the heat.

When the water has been absorbed, remove the plastic wrap and fluff up the couscous with a fork.

Put the yoghurt, icing sugar, Turkish delight and saffron in a bowl and mix to combine.

Keep the elements in their separate bowls in the fridge until ready to serve. To assemble, use glasses or jars so that you can see the layers. Put 2–3 tablespoonfuls of the couscous in each glass, then spoon in the yoghurt mixture and top with the berry mixture.

Turkey meat is an underrated ingredient, and the combination of it with the crisp latkes and poached eggs works well to make a beautiful breakfast dish. Growing up in Israel, we always thought that smoked turkey was ham.

HERB & POTATO LATKES WITH POACHED EGGS & TURKEY

MAKES 12 (SERVES 4)

1 kg (2 lb 4 oz) desiree
 (all-purpose) potatoes,
 peeled and coarsely grated
5 egg whites
50 g (1¾ oz) potato flour
1 handful flat-leaf (Italian) parsley,
 leaves finely chopped
1 small handful dill, finely chopped
30 g (1 oz/¼ cup) finely chopped
 spring onions (scallions)
125 ml (4 fl oz/½ cup) light olive oil
8 eggs, poached
12 slices good-quality turkey breast
1 handful rocket (arugula) leaves,
 to serve

Rinse the grated potato under cold running water to remove the excess starch and drain well. Put the potato in a tea towel (dish towel) and twist and squeeze to remove any remaining water.

Transfer the potato to a large bowl and add the egg whites, potato flour, parsley, dill and spring onion. Season with salt and freshly ground black pepper and mix well. The mixture should have a firm batter consistency.

Heat one-third of the olive oil in a non-stick frying pan over medium heat. To make each latke, drop 2–3 tablespoons of batter into the pan and gently flatten to 1 cm (½ inch) thick. Cook in batches for 2–3 minutes each side, until golden, adding more oil to the pan each time.

Layer 3 latkes per serve with the turkey slices, and serve with 2 eggs each and rocket leaves on the side.

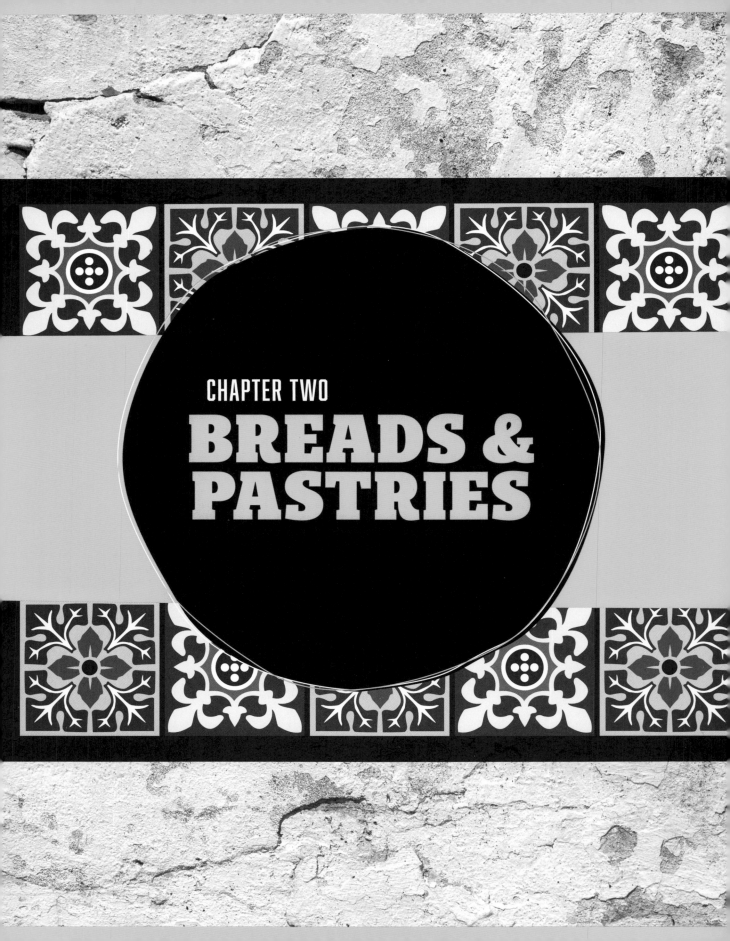

CHAPTER TWO

BREADS & PASTRIES

WE SEE BREAD – ALONG WITH WATER – AS THE BASIS OF LIFE, AND IT SITS AT THE CENTRE OF THE TABLE IN SOME FORM AT EVERY MEAL.

I have included recipes for my favourite classic Middle Eastern breads and pastries, as well as ways to adapt them to suit your tastes and needs. For me, pita bread is the ultimate staple, and once you've mastered it, you can modify the recipe freely – as I have done with the za'atar bread (see page 57). Or simply add an egg and you have egg pita bread. It's that easy.

Bourekas originated in Hungary and have become a classic Israeli street food, where they are often served with tea-soaked eggs. Other variations are made with cheese, spinach and different seeds on top.

BOUREKAS (MIDDLE EASTERN SAUSAGE ROLLS)

MAKES 9

500 g (1 lb 2 oz) coarse minced (ground) beef
40 g (1½ oz) fresh or dry breadcrumbs
2 spring onions (scallions), white part and half of green part finely chopped
1 large handful flat-leaf (Italian) parsley, leaves finely chopped
100 ml (3½ fl oz) extra virgin olive oil
2 eggs, beaten, plus 1 egg, extra, beaten
2 teaspoons sea salt flakes
700 g (1 lb 9 oz) good-quality puff pastry (or 3 purchased puff pastry sheets)
2 tablespoons sesame seeds

Preheat the oven to 190°C (375°F).

Place the beef mince, breadcrumbs, spring onions, parsley, olive oil, 2 eggs and the salt in a large bowl. Season with freshly ground black pepper and mix by hand to combine.

If using a block of pastry, roll it out until 5 mm (¼ inch) thick, into sheets about 20 cm x 20 cm (8 inch by 8 inch). Cut each pastry sheet into thirds. If using purchased pastry sheets, cut them into thirds.

Brush the pastry sheets with the extra beaten egg. Put 2–3 tablespoons of the minced beef mixture along one of the long edges of the pastry. Roll into a long sausage shape, then shape like a snail shell. Repeat until you have used all of the pastry and the mince filling.

Place the bourekas onto a baking tray lined with baking paper, leaving enough room for a little spreading. Brush the tops with beaten egg and sprinkle over the sesame seeds. Bake for 35 minutes, or until golden brown.

Serve with tea-soaked eggs (pictured right, see page 18), if desired.

Challah is good if you are looking for something a little lighter than brioche. If you do want a richer dough, use warm milk instead of the warm water.

CHALLAH BREAD

MAKES 1 LARGE LOAF

500 g (1 lb 2 oz/3⅓ cups) strong flour, sifted, plus extra for dusting
1 x 7 g (¼ oz) dry yeast sachet
½ teaspoon salt
3 tablespoons raw (demerara) sugar
2 egg yolks, plus 1 extra egg yolk, beaten with a few drops of milk or oil, for brushing
4 tablespoons rice bran or vegetable oil
250 ml (9 fl oz/1 cup) warm water

Line a baking tray with baking paper.

Put the flour, yeast, salt and sugar in a large bowl and mix to combine. Make a well in the centre and add the 2 egg yolks, rice bran oil and half (125 ml/4 fl oz/½ cup) of the water. Using your hands, bring the flour into the liquid and mix to a sticky dough. Add more water as required.

Dust a work surface with extra flour and knead the dough for 3–5 minutes, or until smooth.

Put the dough in a clean bowl and cover with a damp tea towel (dish towel) or plastic wrap with a few holes pricked in it. Leave the dough to rise for 45 minutes, or until it has doubled in size.

Divide the dough into 3 equal sized balls. Lightly knead each ball to knock out the air. Leave the dough balls on the work surface covered with the damp tea towel for another 30 minutes, or until doubled in size.

Knead each ball lightly again to knock out the air for 1–2 minutes. Dust the work surface with more flour if necessary and roll the balls into equal sized long logs. Line the 3 logs up side-by-side and press the top ends together to secure. Plait the dough loosely. Press the ends together to secure and tuck underneath.

Transfer the plaited dough to the baking tray. Cover with a damp tea towel and leave to rise for 30 minutes, or until the dough has doubled in size.

Preheat the oven to 170°C (325°F). With a pastry brush, brush the top of the bread with the egg yolk and oil/milk mixture. Bake for 35–45 minutes, or until golden brown.

*I love these biscuits. You can make them whatever size you like –
bite-sized if you are serving them with dips, olives or cheese, or
larger if you would like them as a snack on their own. The dough logs
can be stored in the freezer and then cut and cooked when required.*

SEA SALT & ZA'ATAR BISCUITS

MAKES 24

*210 g (7 ½ oz) plain (all-purpose)
    flour, plus extra for dusting*
*150 g (5½ oz) cold butter, cut
    into cubes*
1 teaspoon sea salt
*1 teaspoon za'atar (see page 214),
    plus 3 teaspoons extra
    to garnish*
½ teaspoon baking powder
*100 g (3½ oz) haloumi
    cheese, grated*
1 egg, whisked
*2 tablespoons sesame seeds,
    to garnish*

Put the flour, butter, sea salt, 1 teaspoon of za'atar, baking powder and
haloumi in a food processor. Mix until a crumb-like consistency.

Lightly dust a work surface with flour. Transfer the mixture to the
work surface and, using your hands, combine and work into a large
ball of dough. Roll the dough into a log shape the size of the biscuit
you want. Wrap the log in plastic wrap and chill in the fridge for
2 hours, or until firm.

Preheat the oven to 170°C (325°F). Line a baking tray with baking
paper. Cut the firm chilled log into 1 cm (½ inch) thick rounds
(or whatever thickness you desire). Put on the baking tray and
brush with the whisked egg. Scatter over the sesame seeds and
extra za'atar. Bake for 20 minutes, or until lightly golden brown.
Cool on the baking tray.

The biscuits will last for 5 days in an airtight container.

The basic bread used all around the Middle East, pita bread is delicious with hummus and can be filled with just about anything you like. The dough can be used in many other recipes and cut to whatever size or shape you like.

PITA BREAD

MAKES 8 PITA BREADS

500 g (1 lb 2 oz/3⅓ cups) strong
    bread flour, sifted, plus extra
    for dusting
1 x 7 g (¼ oz) dry yeast sachet
1 tablespoon sea salt flakes
2½ tablespoons extra virgin olive oil
350 ml (12 fl oz) warm water

Put the flour, yeast and salt in a large bowl and mix to combine. Make a well in the centre and slowly add the olive oil. Using your hands, combine the flour and oil. Gradually add the warm water until the dough is a little sticky (you may not need to use all of it). The dough will come together when you start kneading it.

Dust a work surface with flour and knead the dough for 3–4 minutes, until it forms a nice smooth consistency.

Put the dough in a clean bowl and cover with a damp tea towel (dish towel) or plastic wrap with a few holes pricked in it. Leave in a warm place to rise for 1 hour, or until doubled in size.

Cut the dough into 8 equal pieces. Roll each piece of dough into a ball (or whatever shape you like). Dust the work surface with extra flour, place the 8 balls of dough on it and cover with the damp tea towel or plastic wrap with holes to rise again for 30 minutes.

Roll out each ball of dough into a circle about 5 mm (¼ inch) thick, or whatever thickness you like. Leave to rest for 20 minutes.

Preheat the oven to 180°C (350°F). Line a baking tray with baking paper or preheat a pizza stone (they give the bread a nice colour).

Put the dough circles on the baking tray or pizza stone (you may need to cook them in batches) and bake for 10–15 minutes, or until a light colour. Allow to cool on a tea towel so the pita breads do not lose too much moisture. Use within 1–2 days. These pita breads can also be frozen, as soon as they have been cooled, for up to 3 weeks.

Both savoury and sweet, this bread is delicious eaten with a dollop of Greek-style yoghurt, or slow-roasted tomatoes and feta cheese. You can also make it with eggplant (aubergine) instead of cauliflower.

ROASTED CAULIFLOWER & RAISIN UPSIDE-DOWN BREAD

SERVES 8–10

500 g (1 lb 2 oz/3⅓ cups) strong flour, plus extra for dusting
1 x 7 g (¼ oz) dry yeast sachet
1 tablespoon sea salt flakes
2½ tablespoons olive oil
350 ml (12 fl oz) warm water
1 large cauliflower, cut into large florets
1½ tablespoons ground cumin
100 g (3½ oz) raisins
oil spray for cooking

Mix the flour, yeast and salt in a large bowl. Make a well in the centre and slowly add the olive oil. Using your hands, combine the flour and oil. Gradually add enough of the warm water to make a slightly sticky dough. Dust a work surface with extra flour and knead the dough for 3–5 minutes until smooth. Put the dough in a clean bowl and cover with a damp tea towel (dish towel) or plastic wrap with a few holes pricked in it. Leave in a warm place to rise for 1 hour or until doubled in size.

Meanwhile, preheat the oven to 180°C (350°F), line a baking tray with baking paper and bring a large saucepan of water to the boil. Add the cauliflower to the saucepan and cook for 2–3 minutes. Drain and transfer to a large bowl. Add the cumin, salt and freshly ground black pepper to the cauliflower and mix well. Transfer to the baking tray and cook for 20–25 minutes, until the cauliflower is coloured. Remove the cauliflower and leave the oven on.

Put the raisins and 100 ml (3½ fl oz) water in a small saucepan over medium heat. Simmer until the water has been absorbed. Set aside.

Spray a round 24 cm (9½ in) cake tin with cooking oil spray and line the base with baking paper. Dust a work surface with flour and roll the dough into a round the same size as the cake tin (the dough will be fairly thick).

Add the raisins to the cauliflower, combine and scatter over the base of the cake tin. Put the dough on top and gently tuck in the sides. Allow to rest for 20–25 minutes, until the dough has doubled in size again.

Bake for 40 minutes, or until nicely coloured. Cool in the tin for 5 minutes. Turn out onto a serving board. Serve at room temperature.

They might not be exactly Middle Eastern, but cinnamon buns have a certain spicy and sticky affinity with the pastries we love. Enjoy one mid-morning or mid-afternoon with a cup of tea.

STICKY PECAN CINNAMON BUNS

MAKES 12

100 g (3½ oz) butter
250 ml (9 fl oz/1 cup) full-cream (whole) milk
650 g (1 lb 7 oz/4⅓ cups) plain (all-purpose) flour, sifted, plus extra for dusting
2 x 7 g (¼ oz) dry yeast sachets
1 teaspoon salt
2 eggs

FILLING

50 g (1¾ oz) butter, at room temperature, coarsely chopped
250 g (9 oz) dark brown sugar
2 teaspoons ground cinnamon

GLAZE

50 g (1¾ oz) butter
350 ml (12 fl oz) maple syrup
150 g (5½ oz/1½ cups) pecans, coarsely chopped

Heat the butter and milk in a small saucepan over medium heat until the butter has melted. Set aside to cool.

Put the sifted flour and yeast in the bowl of an electric stand mixer. Using the paddle attachment, combine the flour and yeast. Add the butter mixture, salt and eggs and mix until a soft dough forms.

Dust a work surface lightly with flour. Knead the dough for 2 minutes, until you have a smooth circular ball, and put it in a clean bowl dusted with flour. Cover with a damp tea towel (dish towel) and set aside in a warm place for 45 minutes, or until the dough has doubled in size.

Meanwhile, make the filling. Put the butter, brown sugar and cinnamon in a bowl and beat until combined. Set aside.

To make the glaze, put the butter and maple syrup in a small saucepan over medium–low heat. Heat until just warm and combined. Line a 20 cm x 30 cm (8 inch x 12 inch) baking tray with baking paper. Pour the glaze over the base of the tray and scatter over the pecans.

Divide the dough into 2 equal portions. Dust a work surface lightly with flour. Take 1 portion and roll it out into a 1 cm (½ inch) thick rectangle. Spread half of the filling over the dough. Take the long side of the dough and roll it into a log shape. Cut into 6 equal portions. Repeat with the remaining dough and filling.

Place the 12 pieces on the baking tray in rows on top of the glaze. Cover with a tea towel and set aside for 45 minutes, or until the dough doubles in size (the buns will most likely be touching each other). Halfway through this rising process, preheat the oven to 180°C (350°F).

Bake for 40–45 minutes. Allow to cool in the tin for 5 minutes only. Turn out onto a serving tray.

While it's not as firm or thick as a store-bought crumpet, this bread is delicious with tagines or any kind of stew because it has a lovely chewy texture and the holes absorb the sauce beautifully. You can adjust the size of the crumpets according to your preference or the size of the pan you are using. Using raw (demerara) sugar will give the bread a rich caramelised flavour, and dark brown sugar will give it a deeper colour.

YEMENITE CRUMPET BREAD

MAKES 8 LARGE OR 16 SMALL CRUMPETS

500 g (1 lb 2 oz/3⅓ cups) plain
    (all-purpose) flour, sifted
1 x 7 g (¼ oz) dry yeast sachet
1 tablespoon raw (demerara) or
    dark brown sugar
2 teaspoons sea salt flakes
650 ml (22½ fl oz) warm water
oil spray for cooking

Put the flour, yeast, sugar and salt in a mixing bowl and whisk to combine (whisking will give a smoother texture). Pour the warm water over the dry ingredients and whisk until you have a silky yet wet and gluggy mixture.

Cover the bowl with a damp tea towel (dish towel) or plastic wrap with a few holes pricked in it. Put the bowl in a warm place and allow to rest for 1–1½ hours, or until the volume has doubled.

Spray a 22–24 cm (8½–9½ inch) non-stick frying pan with cooking oil spray while the pan is cold. Gently ladle in the batter until it covers the base of the pan and is about 5 mm (¼ inch) in thickness. Turn the heat to low and cover the pan with a lid. Cook the crumpet for 4–5 minutes. Check that the bottom of the crumpet is cooked and has a very light golden colour. Once cooked, gently remove the crumpet from the pan and put it onto a plate. Don't flip the crumpet over as you want to retain as much of the aeration as possible.

To cook the remaining crumpets you will need to make sure the frying pan has completely cooled down each time, and then repeat the process until all of the mixture is used. Keep the cooked crumpets warm or serve at room temperature.

Crumpet bread is best eaten on the day it is cooked but will last for 2–3 days. The bread can be frozen, as soon as it has been cooked and cooled, for up to 3 weeks.

For an easy-to-make cheat's version of the traditional bagel, you can't go past these.

MINI FENNEL SEED BAGELS

MAKES 8

350 g (12 oz/2⅓ cups) strong flour, plus extra for dusting
1 x 7 g (¼ oz) dry yeast sachet
120 ml (3¾ fl oz) light olive oil
180 ml (5¾ fl oz) dry white wine
1½ teaspoons salt
1 teaspoon fennel seeds, toasted and crushed
1 egg, whisked, for egg wash
2 teaspoons fennel seeds, extra, to garnish
sea salt flakes, to garnish

Sift the flour into a large mixing bowl. Add the yeast and mix to combine. Add the olive oil, wine, salt and toasted fennel seeds and mix until combined. Lightly knead the dough for just 1–2 minutes – do not overknead as you want the dough to be short and dense.

Roll the dough into a ball and put it into a clean bowl, cover with a tea towel (dish towel) and leave to rise for 2 hours in a warm place.

After 2 hours the dough will have increased in size (but do not expect it to have doubled because of its oiliness and dense texture).

Line a baking tray with baking paper. Dust a work surface with flour and cut the dough into 8 equal portions. Roll each one into a sausage shape and bring the ends together to form a circle. Place the bagels on the baking tray. Cover with a tea towel and leave in a warm place to rise for 30 minutes.

Preheat the oven to 180°C (350°F).

Paint the egg wash onto the bagels with a pastry brush. Sprinkle with the fennel seeds and sea salt flakes. Bake for 25 minutes, until golden.

Great served with stews, these roti are also delicious for breakfast with grated tomato, chilli and hard-boiled eggs. The dough needs to be rested overnight, so this recipe is made over 2 days.

YEMENITE PAN ROTI

MAKES 8 ROTIS

500 g (1 lb 2 oz/3⅓ cups) plain (all-purpose) flour, sifted, plus extra for dusting
20 g (¾ oz) dark brown sugar
1 teaspoon salt
200 g (7 oz) butter, melted and cooled, plus extra for greasing
oil spray for cooking
olive oil or clarified butter, for cooking

Put the flour, sugar and salt in a bowl and mix to combine. Slowly add 400 ml (14 fl oz) water until you have a soft but not too sticky dough.

Dust a work surface lightly with flour and knead the dough for 5 minutes, or until you have a smooth ball. Alternatively, you can mix the dough using an electric stand mixer with a dough hook for 2–3 minutes (do not overmix). Wrap the dough in plastic wrap and let it rest in the fridge for at least 2 hours.

Divide the dough into 8 equal-sized balls. Using your hands, spread some of the melted butter onto a work surface. Coat your palms with more melted butter and stretch the dough as thinly as possible into rectangles using both hands, then brush melted butter over the dough.

Fold the long edges of the stretched dough into the centre, then fold the shorter edges into the centre and you should have a small rectangular shape. Repeat this process at least 2–3 times. (You are trying to create layering as you would in puff pastry.) Repeat with each ball of dough.

Spray a baking tray with cooking oil. Put the dough balls on the tray, cover with plastic wrap and let the dough rest overnight in the fridge.

When ready to cook the roti, grease the work surface with extra melted butter. Stretch out each dough ball to approximately 20 cm (8 inches) in diameter on the greased surface.

Heat a frying pan with a lid to medium-low heat. Add 1 teaspoon of olive oil or clarified butter to the pan and add the stretched dough. Put the lid on the pan and cook until lightly golden, approximately 4–5 minutes each side.

These roti are best eaten on the day they are cooked, but can be made in advance and warmed just before serving.

When I was a kid, there was a bakery close to our house and on the weekends we used to go there for fresh pita and za'atar bread. But by the time we got home, we would have eaten most of it – I mean, who can resist freshly baked bread? The smell of this bread cooking is the true smell of the Middle East.

ZA'ATAR BREAD

MAKES 8 BREADS

1 quantity pita bread dough
   (see page 47)
8 tablespoons za'atar (see page 214)
150 ml (5 fl oz) good-quality olive oil

Make the dough according to the instructions on page 47. Once you've rolled the balls of dough into rounds and set them aside to rest for 20 minutes, preheat the oven to 180°C (350°F) and line a baking tray with baking paper.

Put the za'atar and olive oil in a bowl. Mix to combine.

Gently stamp your fingers into the dough rounds, making little valleys just deep enough so the za'atar oil won't roll off the dough. (Don't press too hard as you want the dough to remain aerated.) Spoon the za'atar oil over the dough.

Put the dough circles on the baking tray (you may need to cook them in batches) and bake for 10–15 minutes, or until a light colour. Allow to cool on a tea towel (dish towel) and use within 1–2 days.

CHAPTER THREE

A LITTLE SOMETHING TO EAT

PERHAPS YOU WANT SOMETHING TO SNACK ON, A DISH THAT IS QUICK TO PREPARE OR MAYBE A LIGHT MEAL?

Here is a collection of light bites, skewers, hand-around food and small-but-perfectly-formed meals. Some of these delicious dishes work well on their own, and others are ideal as components of a larger feast served as part of your shared table.

I like to use metal skewers as they retain their heat and cook the centre of the chicken, but you can certainly use bamboo skewers soaked in water for a few minutes before threading on the chicken, which will keep the skewers from burning on the barbecue.

CHICKEN CHERMOULA

SERVES 4 AS A MAIN

1 kg (2 lb 4 oz) boneless, skinless chicken thighs, cut into 3 cm x 3 cm (1¼ inch x 1¼ inch) pieces
4 tablespoons chermoula (see page 220)
2 tablespoons extra virgin olive oil
1 teaspoon sea salt flakes
1 tablespoon chopped coriander (cilantro) leaves

Put the chicken pieces in a large bowl. Add the chermoula, olive oil, salt and coriander and stir to combine. Cover and put in the fridge for 30 minutes to marinate.

Thread 3–4 pieces of chicken onto each skewer. Set aside until ready to cook.

Heat the barbecue to high and brush the grill with oil so the skewers won't stick. Cook the skewers for 3–4 minutes on each side.

Vegetarians will love this beautiful dish. It is best to make this when the truss tomatoes are in season and full of flavour. Serve it as a side dish or as a main course with a salad.

HERB & RICE-STUFFED TOMATOES

SERVES 6

12 truss tomatoes
3 tablespoons light olive oil
1 small brown onion, finely diced,
　　plus 1 small brown onion, extra,
　　finely diced
200 g (7 oz/1 cup) long-grain or
　　basmati rice
1 teaspoon sea salt
¼ teaspoon freshly crushed
　　black pepper
375 ml (13 fl oz/1½ cups) boiling
　　chicken stock or water
70 g (2½ oz) pine nuts,
　　lightly toasted
1 large handful mixed herbs (such
　　as mint, flat-leaf (Italian) parsley
　　and dill)
3 teaspoons olive oil
1 teaspoon dried mint

Cut the tops off the tomatoes and keep the tomato lids with the green stalks attached to be used later. Using a spoon, scoop out the flesh of the tomatoes and set aside for the sauce. You will be left with the shell of the tomato.

To make the filling, heat the light olive oil in a medium saucepan over medium heat. Add 1 diced onion and cook for 2–3 minutes. Add the rice and cook, tossing constantly, for 2–3 minutes. Add the salt, pepper and boiling stock or water. Bring to the boil, cover with a lid, reduce the heat to low and cook for 18 minutes.

Remove the pan from the heat and stir through the pine nuts and herbs.

Stuff the tomatoes with the rice filling and set aside.

Preheat the oven to 180°C (350°F).

Coarsely chop the tomato flesh.

Heat the olive oil in a 6–10 cm/2¼–4 inch deep ovenproof frying pan or baking tray. Add the extra onion and cook for 3–4 minutes. Add the tomato flesh and cook for 5 minutes. Add the dried mint and season with salt and freshly ground black pepper. Carefully transfer the stuffed tomatoes to this pan and cover with their tomato lids.

Roast in the oven for 30–35 minutes, until the tomatoes have a roasted colour.

Gather six 125 ml (4 fl oz/½ cup) preserving jars, available from kitchenware stores, for the pâté. It's important to have the chicken livers, eggs and butter at room temperature or the mixture may curdle. You'll need to begin this recipe a day before you want to eat the pâté.

CHICKEN LIVER PÂTÉ

MAKES ABOUT 1 KG (2 LB 4 OZ)

500 g (1 lb 2 oz) chicken
    livers, trimmed
milk, for soaking chicken livers
1 tablespoon olive oil
½ small onion, sliced
2½ tablespoons red wine
3 eggs, at room temperature
1 teaspoon brandy
1 teaspoon caster (superfine) sugar
1 teaspoon salt
350 g (12 oz) unsalted butter,
    softened and chopped
tomato & baharat jam (see page
    223) and crisp pita bread
    (see page 227), to serve

Put the livers in a bowl and pour over enough milk to cover. Cover the bowl and refrigerate overnight.

Drain the livers and bring to room temperature. Preheat the oven to 100°C (200°F).

Heat the olive oil in a small frying pan over low heat. Add the onion and cook for 3 minutes, or until softened. Increase the heat to medium, add the wine and cook for 3–4 minutes, or until caramelised. Remove the pan from the heat and allow the onion to cool.

Put the onion, livers, eggs, brandy, sugar and salt in a large bowl. Blend using a stick blender until very smooth. With the motor on high speed, gradually add 200 g (7 oz) of the butter, one piece at a time, blending until smooth and creamy (if the mixture is clumpy, keep blending on high speed until smooth). Strain through a fine sieve into a bowl.

Pour 100 ml (3½ fl oz) of the mixture into each jar. Seal with the lids and put the jars in a deep roasting tin. Add enough hot water to the tin to come halfway up the sides of the jars. Place in the oven and cook for 25–30 minutes, or until the pâté is just set.

Remove the jars from the tin, release the lids and allow to cool slightly. Chill the jars of pâté in the fridge for 2 hours.

Meanwhile, put the remaining 150 g (5½ oz) of the butter in a saucepan over low heat, skimming any foam from the surface as it melts, but not stirring. When melted, remove from the heat and allow to stand for 1 minute so the milk solids settle to the bottom.

Pour the clarified butter into a bowl and discard the milk solids in the pan. Allow to cool slightly. Pour 5 mm (¼ inch) clarified butter over the pâté in each jar. Secure the lids and put in the fridge for 4 hours. Serve with the tomato & baharat jam and crisp pita bread.

There is nothing that chicken soup can't heal, it is said, and it's one of those dishes you can eat at any time of the day.

CHICKEN, NOODLE & LEEK SOUP

SERVES 4-6

3 tablespoons olive oil
2 garlic cloves, crushed
1 leek, white part and half
    of the green part, rinsed
    and thinly sliced
100 g (3½ oz) kugel, egg or
    vermicelli noodles
sea salt and white pepper, to season
1 small handful flat-leaf (Italian)
    parsley, finely chopped

STOCK

1 small (about 1.2 kg/2 lb 10 oz)
    chicken
1 brown onion, finely chopped
3 garlic cloves, crushed
2 celery stalks
1 carrot
2 fresh or dried bay leaves
5 garlic cloves, extra
½ teaspoon white peppercorns

To make the stock, put all of the ingredients in a large saucepan with 5 litres (175 fl oz/20 cups) water. Cook over medium heat for 45 minutes.

Remove the saucepan from the heat and transfer the chicken to a chopping board. When cool enough to handle, pull the chicken meat off the carcass and shred with your hands. Cover and set aside until you are ready to serve the soup. Discard the chicken carcass. Strain the stock and set aside. Discard the vegetables.

To make the soup, put the olive oil and garlic in a large saucepan over medium heat and cook for 1–2 minutes. Add the leek and cook for 3–4 minutes. Add 1 litre (35 fl oz/4 cups) of the reserved chicken stock. Turn the heat up to high and bring to the boil. Add the noodles and cook according to the packet instructions, or approximately 5 minutes, stirring from time to time.

Add the shredded chicken to the noodle stock and cook for 4–5 minutes, just to warm through and meld the flavours. Season with sea salt and white pepper. Stir through the parsley and serve.

*It is so easy to put this dish together, and yet it makes such
a big impact with its sharp, clean flavours.*

DUKKAH LAMB CUTLETS WITH MINT & POMEGRANATE SALAD

SERVES 4

3 tablespoons olive oil
6 tablespoons hazelnut dukkah
    (see page 212)
8 large lamb cutlets (or lamb chops
    or noisettes)

MINT & POMEGRANATE SALAD
1 handful mint leaves
4 tablespoons pomegranate seeds
1 preserved lemon (see page 216),
    skin only, julienned
juice of ½ a lemon
3 tablespoons olive oil

Put the olive oil and dukkah in a large bowl and mix together. Add the lamb and rub the dukkah mixture into the meat. Cover the bowl and transfer to the fridge to marinate for 30 minutes.

To make the salad, put the mint, pomegranate seeds and preserved lemon in a bowl. Shake together the lemon juice and olive oil in a small jar. Pour over the salad, toss gently and season with salt and freshly ground black pepper, taking care not to use too much salt as there is salt in the dukkah on the cutlets.

Heat the barbecue to high or heat a chargrill pan over high heat on your stovetop. Cook the lamb cutlets for 2–3 minutes on each side. Remove the pan from the heat and rest the lamb for 5 minutes before serving with the mint and pomegranate salad.

CLASSIC MIDDLE EASTERN FEAST

Everything here is a perfect 'little something to eat' that can be gathered together to create a banquet. And everything on this table is what I'd expect to be served when I'm invited to a Middle Eastern household for a meal – pita or za'atar bread, tabouleh, fresh vegetable dishes, a variety of skewers and a meat dish. Along with the signature dishes in this book, we have added a plate of sliced truss tomatoes sprinkled with olive oil, salt and freshly ground black pepper, and crisp pita bread (deep-fry pita bread in hot oil for a minute or two and drain on paper towel, see page 227 – it's delicious). And, of course, we would also have hummus. It wouldn't be a Middle Eastern feast without the hummus …

Whether you cook them on a barbecue or in the oven, you'll love these sardines wrapped in vine leaves. You can buy pickled vine leaves from Middle Eastern grocery stores, and fresh ones at farmers' markets, or you may have a friend who has a grapevine at home. If you are using fresh vine leaves, you'll need to blanch them in boiling salted water for 2–3 minutes, or until they change colour. Refresh in icy cold water and pat dry with paper towel.

GRILLED SARDINES WITH HARISSA

SERVES 4

16 sardines
6 teaspoons red harissa
   (see page 222), plus extra,
   to serve
16 large or 32 small vine leaves
3 tablespoons olive oil
lemon wedges, to serve

Cut a slit in the belly of the sardines, or ask your fishmonger to do this for you. Rinse in cold water and pat dry. Rub the sardines with the harissa, inside and out.

Depending on the size of the vine leaf you are using, lay 1 or 2 leaves on a work surface, place a sardine on the diagonal and wrap. It is okay if the head and tail are poking out at either end. Rub the vine leaf parcels with the olive oil and season with salt and freshly ground black pepper.

Heat the barbecue to medium–high and cook the vine-wrapped sardines for 2–3 minutes on each side. Alternatively, you can cook them on a baking tray for 8–10 minutes in an oven preheated to 180°C (350°F). If cooking in the oven, you will not need to turn the vine-wrapped sardines.

Serve with lemon wedges and extra red harissa on the side.

'Neah' means 'raw' in Arabic, and this is the equivalent to the French steak tartare – which, as a chef, I like, because you can see the ingredients and the quality of the meat being served. I also think presenting this dish using a deconstructed approach is an elegant way to start a meal. In fact, it's a real showstopper. As you will be eating the meat raw, I recommend using only the best quality lamb for optimal flavour. I'd also just like to mention the burghul – it may seem like only a small quantity, but it will triple in size when blanched.

KIBBEH NEAH

SERVES 4

40 g (1½ oz) burghul (bulgur)
80 g (2¾ oz/⅔ cup) walnuts,
    finely crushed
2 tablespoons finely chopped
    flat-leaf (Italian) parsley
1 tablespoon finely chopped basil,
    plus extra leaves to garnish
1 teaspoon ground cumin
1 teaspoon ground cinnamon
1 teaspoon sea salt flakes
good-quality extra virgin olive oil,
    to drizzle
280 g (10 oz) good-quality lean
    lamb fillet or backstrap, cleaned
2 tablespoons pomegranate
    molasses (see page 229)
crisp pita bread (see page 227) or
    lavosh, to serve

Put the burghul in a bowl and rinse with plenty of hot water. Leave to soak for 2–3 minutes in hot water. Drain the burghul in a sieve or strainer with small holes, pressing down lightly to remove the water. Spread the burghul out evenly on a baking tray and allow it to steam and cool to room temperature. Fluff up the burghul using your hands.

Put the burghul, walnuts, parsley, basil, cumin, cinnamon and half the salt in a large bowl. Add a drizzle of olive oil and combine gently with your hands. Set aside.

You can prepare the meat using the mincer attachment of an electric mixer set to the coarse setting. Alternatively, you can mince the meat by hand using a very sharp knife. Gently combine the minced lamb with the remaining salt and a drizzle of olive oil, taking care not to overmix. Set aside.

Spread out the seasoned burghul mixture on a serving plate. Create a sausage shape with the lamb mince and lay it over the burghul. Drizzle the pomegranate molasses and some olive oil over the lamb and burghul.

At the table, gently mix the burghul and lamb mince together with two forks. Garnish with basil leaves and serve with crisp pita bread or lavosh.

Including your guests in the preparation of a meal is a great way to entertain, and these burgers are ideal for a lunch party where you get the ingredients ready beforehand, and lay them on the table for all to make their own.

LAMB BURGERS WITH MIDDLE EASTERN COLESLAW

SERVES 4

750 g (1 lb 10 oz) good-quality
    coarse minced (ground) lamb
2 teaspoons coriander seeds,
    toasted and crushed
1 handful coriander (cilantro),
    leaves finely chopped
3 tablespoons olive oil
5 tablespoons red harissa
    (see page 222)
1 teaspoon chilli flakes
4 tablespoons aïoli (see page 226),
    to serve
4 brioche burger buns, toasted
Middle Eastern coleslaw (see
    page 94), to serve

Put the minced lamb, coriander seeds, chopped coriander, olive oil, 4 tablespoons of the harissa and the chilli flakes in a large bowl. Season with salt and freshly ground black pepper and mix to combine.

Divide the meat mixture into four equal portions and gently shape into burger patties with your hands. (Don't overwork the patties as the meat will become tough.)

Cook the burgers in a non-stick frying pan over medium heat for 2–3 minutes each side (for medium–rare), or to your taste. You can also cook them using the grill (broiler) or barbecue heated to medium.

Combine the aïoli and remaining harissa in a small bowl.

To assemble the burgers, toast the cut side of the buns. Place the bun bottoms on plates and add a dollop of the harissa aïoli, a handful of coleslaw and a pattie. Add another handful of coleslaw, another dollop of aïoli and top with the bun lid.

Kids love these, and they make a good meat dish if you are trying to introduce new flavours. When my niece and nephews come over for dinner, they work out how many keftas each person should get and always make sure they eat their share! Luckily this recipe can easily be doubled, tripled ... Serve your kefta with hummus, tabouleh and pita bread for a light meal, or make it part of your shared table.

LAMB KEFTA

SERVES 4-6

500 g (1 lb 2 oz) good-quality
    minced (ground) lamb
75 g (2½ oz) pine nuts
1 teaspoon ground cumin
¼ teaspoon ground cinnamon
1 handful flat-leaf (Italian) parsley
    or coriander (cilantro),
    leaves coarsely chopped
2 tablespoons) good-quality
    olive oil
3 tablespoons olive oil, for frying

Put the minced lamb, pine nuts, cumin, cinnamon, parsley or coriander and good-quality olive oil in a large bowl. Combine well with your hands. Form small round balls of mince mixture then flatten to make a small hamburger shape. Set aside in the fridge until ready to cook.

Heat the olive oil for frying in a large frying pan over medium heat. Cook the kefta in batches for 3 minutes on each side, moving them around in the pan, taking care not to overcook them. Keep the kefta warm on a plate covered with foil until all are cooked.

Serve with hummus (see page 210), tabouleh (see page 112) and pita bread (see page 47).

In my family, we normally serve three or four different types of meat at the shared table, and lamb skewers are always on the menu. But they are also a quick and easy everyday option. You can prepare the skewers in advance and cook them when you get home or when your guests arrive. Serve them with homemade pita bread (see page 47) and a grilled eggplant, yoghurt & rocket salad (see page 103) or Tom's fennel salad (see page 115).

LAMB SKEWERS WITH RAS EL HANOUT

SERVES 4

1 kg (2 lb 4 oz) lamb backstrap, cut into 3 cm x 3 cm (1 inch x 1 inch) cubes
4 tablespoons olive oil
1 tablespoon ras el hanout (see page 213)
2 garlic cloves, crushed
½ teaspoon sea salt flakes
pita bread and salad, to serve

Put the lamb, olive oil, ras el hanout, garlic and salt in a large bowl. Combine to coat the lamb well. Cover and transfer to the fridge to marinate for 30–60 minutes.

Thread 4–5 pieces of lamb onto metal skewers. Cover and refrigerate until ready to cook.

Heat the barbecue to high and cook the lamb skewers for 2 minutes on each side, or until coloured and cooked to your liking. Serve with pita bread and salad.

According to my mum, this 'healing' soup has all the ingredients to make you feel happier and is good to eat when you are not feeling 100 per cent. She likes to leave her version quite textured, but I blend mine a little to get a smoother consistency. I also love making a richer version by adding 2 tablespoons of butter at the end. You can garnish this soup with croutons, shredded chicken or grated kashkaval cheese to make it fancier, but a sprinkle of parsley is just as good.

MUM'S RED LENTIL SOUP

SERVES 8-10

4 tablespoons olive oil
1 brown onion, finely chopped
4 garlic cloves, crushed
4 carrots, grated
1 zucchini (courgette), grated
2 litres (70 fl oz/8 cups) chicken
   or vegetable stock
155 g (5½ oz/¾ cup) red lentils,
   washed and drained
55 g (2 oz/¼ cup) short-grain white
   rice, washed and drained
2 teaspoons ground turmeric
2 teaspoons ground cumin
chilli flakes (optional)
1 large handful flat-leaf
   (Italian) parsley, leaves
   coarsely chopped

Put the olive oil in a large saucepan over medium heat. Add the onion and garlic and cook for 5 minutes, but do not allow to colour. Add the carrot and cook for 3 minutes, then add the zucchini and cook for 1 minute.

Add the stock, lentils and rice and bring to the boil. Reduce the temperature to medium–low and cook for 25–30 minutes, or until the lentils have disintegrated and the other ingredients are starting to break down.

Add the turmeric and cumin and cook for 5 minutes to balance out the flavours. Season with salt, freshly ground black pepper and chilli flakes, if you like a bit more of a kick. Remove from the heat, add the parsley and serve.

I first made this soup with the kabocha variety of pumpkin – the one that has dark green skin with light green stripes, and is also known as buttercup squash or Japanese pumpkin. We were given it by our friends Sally and Hollie, and it had come from Hollie's hometown of Macksville in New South Wales, where they refer to pumpkins as potkins.

PUMPKIN SOUP

SERVES 4

3 tablespoons olive oil
1 brown onion, finely chopped
1 leek, washed and white part
    finely chopped
2 garlic cloves, crushed
1 teaspoon fennel seeds
1 teaspoon ground cumin
1 teaspoon ground coriander
1.2 kg (2 lb 10 oz) pumpkin, peeled
    and cut into chunks
1.25 litres (44 fl oz/5 cups)
    chicken stock
red harissa (see page 222) and
    homemade yoghurt (see page
    231), to serve
coriander (cilantro) leaves,
    to garnish

Put the olive oil in a large deep saucepan over medium heat. Add the onion, leek and garlic and cook for 5 minutes, or until softened but not coloured. Add the fennel seeds, cumin and coriander and cook for 2 minutes. Add the chopped pumpkin and mix well. Add the stock and simmer for 45 minutes, or until the pumpkin is tender.

Remove the pan from the heat and blitz with a stick blender until smooth. To serve, add a dollop of harissa and yoghurt, and scatter over the coriander leaves.

The idea of stuffing seafood, meat and vegetables really appeals to me because it adds an extra surprise to the meal.

STUFFED BABY SQUID WITH SUMAC & PRAWNS

SERVES 6-8

4 tablespoons olive oil
2 small brown onions, chopped
4 garlic cloves, crushed
1 green chilli, finely chopped
200 g (7 oz) prawns, peeled,
    deveined and diced
1 kg (2 lb 4 oz) squid (weight
    before cleaning), around
    10 cm (4 inch) long, cleaned,
    heads chopped
2 handfuls flat-leaf (Italian) parsley,
    leaves chopped
1 tablespoon sumac
1 teaspoon salt

MARINADE
1 tablespoon chopped flat-leaf
    (Italian) parsley
1 tablespoon sumac
5 tablespoons olive oil

Heat the olive oil in a frying pan over medium heat. Add the onion, garlic and chilli and cook for 3–4 minutes. Add the prawn meat and chopped squid heads and cook for 1 minute, just to get some colour, but not to cook through.

Remove the frying pan from the heat and add the parsley, sumac and salt. Allow to cool to room temperature.

Stuff the squid tubes with the filling to three-quarters full. Thread a toothpick through the end to keep the stuffing inside.

To make the marinade, put the parsley, sumac and olive oil in a bowl and season to taste. Add the stuffed squid tubes and marinate for 10–15 minutes in the fridge.

When you are ready to cook, heat the barbecue to high. Cook the stuffed squid tubes for 2 minutes on each side. When serving, remove the toothpick.

CHAPTER FOUR

SALADS & VEGETABLES

MIDDLE EASTERN RECIPES HAVE ALWAYS FEATURED PLENTY OF VEGETABLES, AS THEY ARE SO AFFORDABLE AND ACCESSIBLE.

Animals were kept in the family garden to provide milk and eggs – not meat – and the emphasis was very much on homegrown vegetables. We had a large platter of vegetables, cut and ready to eat, as a snack when we got home from school, which we'd eat straight from the fridge with hummus. The recipes in this chapter are flexible and forgiving. If you don't like an ingredient, you can leave it out and add more of another. And use more or less lemon, oil or spices to suit your taste. Enjoy the process and the end result.

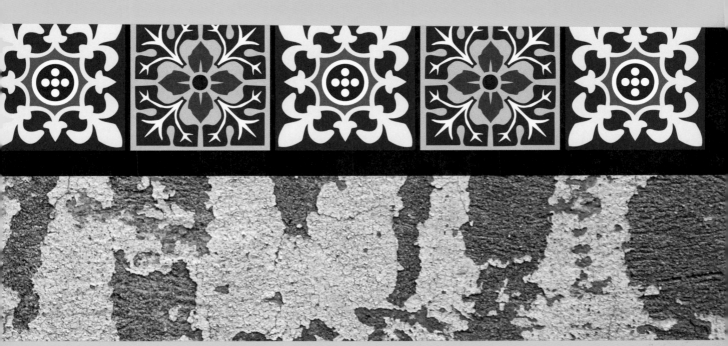

If you want to know how spring tastes and looks on a plate, this is it. Serve this salad with anything and enjoy the way it instantly makes you feel healthy and happy.

BROAD BEAN, TOMATO & CUMIN SEED SALAD

SERVES 4-6 AS A SIDE DISH

500 g (1 lb 2 oz) broad beans

200 g (7 oz) mixed heirloom
    cherry tomatoes, halved

1 large green chilli, seeds removed,
    finely diced

1 handful coriander (cilantro),
    leaves chopped

1 teaspoon cumin seeds, toasted
    and crushed

1 preserved lemon, skin only
    (see page 216)

3–4 spring onions (scallions),
    chopped

juice of 1 lemon

2½ tablespoons olive oil

Blanch the broad beans by putting them in boiling water for 1–2 minutes. Drain and cool under cold running water, then slip off the skins.

Put the peeled broad beans in a large bowl and add the remaining ingredients. Mix gently to combine.

NOTE

If making this salad in advance, prepare and combine all of the ingredients except the lemon juice and olive oil. Cover and refrigerate, adding the dressing ingredients when you are ready to serve.

A friend of mine used to make this salad as a side dish for dinner every Friday night, and I felt the need to have it on my restaurant's menu too. I've added goat's cheese to give it an elegant edge.

WARM MOROCCAN CARROT SALAD

SERVES 4 AS A SIDE DISH

800 g (1 lb 12 oz) baby carrots,
    trimmed and peeled
2 tablespoons olive oil
1 large green chilli, seeds removed,
    finely chopped
2 garlic cloves, crushed
1 tablespoon honey
1 teaspoon ground cumin
1 teaspoon sumac
50 g (1¾ oz) soft goat's
    cheese, crumbled
1 tablespoon finely chopped
    flat-leaf (Italian) parsley
extra virgin olive oil, to drizzle

Bring a medium saucepan filled with salted water to the boil. Add the carrots and boil for 3 minutes. Drain well.

Heat the olive oil in a large frying pan over medium heat. Add the carrots and cook for 1 minute, or until coated in oil. Add the chilli and garlic and cook for 1 minute, or until fragrant (but not coloured). Add the honey and cook for 1 minute, or until warmed through. Add the cumin and sumac, season to taste and toss well to combine. Remove the pan from the heat and allow the carrots to cool slightly then transfer to a serving plate.

Scatter the goat's cheese and parsley over the carrots and drizzle with extra virgin olive oil.

Perhaps it's because I wasn't forced to eat them as a child that I love brussels sprouts now. And I hope this recipe helps make people who have had a bad experience eating brussels sprouts in the past change their opinion.

BRUSSELS SPROUTS, POMEGRANATE & SOFT FETA SALAD

SERVES 4 AS A SIDE DISH

100 g (3½ oz) Danish feta
2 tablespoons full-cream
    (whole) milk
500 g (1 lb 2 oz) brussels sprouts,
    trimmed and halved
1½ tablespoons olive oil
5 tablespoons pomegranate
    molasses (see page 229)
2 tablespoons chopped flat-leaf
    (Italian) parsley
1 small handful mint leaves
60 g (2¼ oz) pistachio nut kernels,
    coarsely chopped
½ pomegranate, seeds removed
    and reserved
extra virgin olive oil, to drizzle

Put the feta and milk in a food processor and blend until smooth. Transfer to a bowl and set aside in the fridge until ready to use.

Bring a medium saucepan of water to the boil with a pinch of salt. Blanch the brussels sprouts for 30 seconds then drain well.

Heat the olive oil in a medium frying pan over medium heat. Add the brussels sprouts and cook for 3–5 minutes, turning them as little as possible to get a chargrilled effect. Add the pomegranate molasses and cook until the brussels sprouts are caramelised, which should take 3–5 minutes. Remove from the heat.

Put the brussels sprouts in a bowl and season with salt. Add the parsley and mint and mix well. Scatter over the pistachios and pomegranate seeds, and add dollops of the feta mixture. Drizzle with olive oil and serve.

You will need the seeds from the pomegranate for this salad, but any liquid that remains can be used to make a pomegranate mojito (see page 194).

CAULIFLOWER & CRANBERRY SALAD

SERVES 4 AS A SIDE DISH

200 g (7 oz/1 cup) pearl barley
½ cauliflower, cut into
    small florets
1 pomegranate, seeds removed
    and reserved
75 g (2½ oz/½ cup)
    dried cranberries
60 g (2¼ oz/½ cup) chopped
    walnuts, toasted
75 g (2½ oz) chopped
    pistachio nut kernels
2 large handfuls flat-leaf (Italian)
    parsley, leaves chopped
4 mint sprigs, leaves chopped
3 tablespoons olive oil
3 tablespoons white balsamic
    or white wine vinegar
2 tablespoons pomegranate
    molasses (see page 229)

Put the pearl barley in a large saucepan of cold water. Bring to the boil over high heat. Reduce the heat to medium and cook for 40 minutes, or until tender. Drain, refresh in cold water and drain again.

Bring a medium saucepan of water to the boil with a pinch of salt. Blanch the cauliflower for 1 minute. Drain, refresh in cold water and drain again.

Put the pearl barley, cauliflower, pomegranate seeds, cranberries, walnuts, pistachios, parsley and mint in a large bowl. Toss to combine.

Put the olive oil, vinegar and pomegranate molasses in a small bowl. Whisk to combine, season to taste and pour over the cauliflower salad. Mix together gently and serve.

The cauliflower is delicious deep-fried in this dish, but if you'd prefer a healthier version it can be roasted in the oven at 180°C/350°F for about 25 minutes instead.

CAULIFLOWER, RAW TAHINI & ZHOUG SALAD

SERVES 6–8 AS A SIDE DISH

rice bran oil, for deep-frying
1 large cauliflower,
    cut into large florets
sea salt flakes, to season
50 g (1¾ oz) raw tahini
juice of 1 lemon
olive oil, to drizzle
1 large handful coriander (cilantro),
    leaves finely chopped
1 tablespoon cumin seeds, toasted
    and crushed
2 tablespoons green zhoug (see
    page 225) or 1 large green chilli,
    finely chopped

Put enough rice bran oil in a large saucepan over high heat to cover and deep-fry the cauliflower. Heat the oil to 170°C (325°F), or until a cube of bread dropped into the oil turns golden brown in 20 seconds. Working in batches, deep-fry the cauliflower until golden in colour, then drain on paper towel.

When ready to serve, put the cauliflower in a bowl and season with sea salt flakes. Combine the tahini, lemon juice and olive oil in a small bowl and spoon over the cauliflower. Scatter over the coriander leaves, cumin seeds and the zhoug or chilli.

The inspiration for this recipe comes from Kristy's Asian-style coleslaw, but I have Middle-Easternised it. You can add shredded poached chicken if you want to turn it into a whole meal.

MIDDLE EASTERN COLESLAW

SERVES 4-6 AS A SIDE DISH

½ red cabbage
2 carrots
sea salt flakes
1 handful mint, leaves picked
2 large handfuls flat-leaf (Italian)
    parsley, leaves finely chopped
1 handful coriander (cilantro),
    leaves coarsely chopped
100 ml (3½ fl oz) extra virgin
    olive oil
4 tablespoons husroum (verjuice)

Use a mandolin or knife to shave the cabbage finely and julienne the carrots. Place in a large bowl, sprinkle with sea salt flakes and press down on the cabbage and carrot with your hands to soften them.

Add the mint, parsley and coriander to the bowl and mix well. Add the olive oil and husroum, and season with freshly ground black pepper. Toss to combine and serve.

In most Mediterranean cultures, a meal starts with a mezze, a relish or a salad. This Persian eggplant is an example of such a starter, but it also works beautifully as a side with most meat or fish dishes. It can be served warm or cold, you can spread it on toast or eat it with a poached egg for breakfast, or you can have it with leftover roasted meats on a sandwich for lunch. It can also be added to an omelette mixture – it really is a great all-rounder!

PERSIAN EGGPLANT

SERVES 4-6

2 eggplants (aubergines), peeled
    and cut into 2 cm (¾ inch) cubes
2 tablespoons coriander seeds
2 tablespoons cumin seeds
1 tablespoon caraway seeds
vegetable oil, for frying
4 tablespoons olive oil
1 large onion, finely diced
1 large red chilli, diced, with seeds
6 garlic cloves, crushed
1 tablespoon ground paprika
1 tablespoon ground turmeric
3 large tomatoes, diced
1 large handful coriander (cilantro),
    leaves and roots chopped
3 tablespoons lemon juice

Put the eggplant in a colander and sprinkle generously with salt. Set aside for 40 minutes to release the excess liquid. Briefly rinse under cold water and pat dry with a clean tea towel (dish towel).

Meanwhile, heat a small frying pan over medium heat and toast the coriander, cumin and caraway seeds for 2 minutes, or until fragrant. Using a mortar and pestle, slightly crush the toasted seeds (keeping their shape). Set aside.

Put enough vegetable oil to come a third of the way up the side of a large frying pan and put the pan over medium–high heat. When the oil is hot, cook the eggplant in batches until golden brown. Set aside on paper towel to absorb the excess oil.

Put the olive oil in a large saucepan over medium heat and cook the onion, chilli and garlic until translucent. Add the toasted seeds, paprika and turmeric and cook until the liquid has evaporated and the pan is dry. Add the tomato and 3 tablespoons water, reduce the heat to medium–low and simmer for 15 minutes. Add the eggplant and cook for a further 5 minutes. Season with sea salt to taste. Add the chopped coriander leaves and roots and the lemon juice. Stir through and remove from the heat. Serve warm or cold.

Using nuts and dried fruit in a salad adds extra crunch and natural sweetness, taking it to the next level. Don't be afraid to change the ingredients in this salad – make it your own by using different nuts, fruit or even vegetables, a different amount of oil or perhaps adding a completely new ingredient.

CHICKPEA, NUT & DRIED FRUIT SALAD

SERVES 4

450 g (1 lb) tinned chickpeas, drained and crushed
100 g (3½ oz) dates, seeds removed, chopped
100 g (3½ oz) dried cranberries
100 g (3½ oz) hazelnuts, toasted and chopped
100 g (3½ oz) whole almonds, skin on, toasted and chopped
1 handful chervil, coarsely chopped
1 large handful mint, leaves torn
2 small carrots, coarsely grated
1 tablespoon cumin seeds, lightly toasted and crushed
zest and juice of 1 lemon
1 tablespoon honey
125 ml (4 fl oz/½ cup) extra virgin olive oil

Put the chickpeas, dates, cranberries, hazelnuts, almonds, chervil, mint and carrot in a large bowl. Combine well.

Put the cumin seeds, lemon zest and juice, honey and olive oil in a small bowl and whisk together.

Add the dressing to the chickpea mixture and combine. Season with salt and transfer the salad to a serving dish.

Green almonds are available from the beginning of spring. Technically, they are unripe almonds where the shell has not dried out yet. Check they're not too woody before you buy them – the texture should resemble that of an apple when you bite into them. Green almonds are good in salads as they have a fresh and grassy flavour with a wonderful crunch. This salad is great served with grilled fish, seafood, pork or chicken.

GREEN ALMOND & FENNEL SALAD

SERVES 6-8 AS A SIDE DISH

500 g (1 lb 2 oz) green
    almonds, washed
2 small fennel bulbs, trimmed
1 handful dill, chopped
2 garlic cloves, crushed
1 small red onion, thinly sliced
juice of 1 lemon
2½ tablespoons olive oil
100 g (3½ oz) blanched almonds,
    lightly toasted and coarsely
    chopped, to garnish

Slice the green almonds coarsely and put in a large bowl.

Using a mandolin or a very sharp knife, finely shave the fennel bulbs. Add to the bowl with the almonds, along with the dill, garlic and onion.

Shake together the lemon juice and olive oil in a small jar. Pour over the salad and toss to combine.

Scatter over the chopped toasted almonds and serve.

DATE-NIGHT FEAST

This was the first meal I ever made for Kristy. Not being sure how far I could go with my cooking, I tried to play it safe with dishes that weren't too overpowering but still had enough flavour. For people just getting into Middle Eastern food, this is a good start. Just ask Kristy.

1 **LENTIL RICE (MUJADDARA)** see page 138
2 **LAMB KEFTA** see page 76
3 **HUMMUS** see page 210
4 **ISRAELI CHOPPED VEGETABLE SALAD** see page 109

Eggplant is a staple in the Middle East and is used in many ways there. This is a lovely side dish to have at a barbecue or to serve with grilled fish. You can also prepare it as a delicious salad (see note below).

GRILLED EGGPLANT, YOGHURT & ROCKET

SERVES 4 AS A SIDE DISH

2 large eggplants (aubergines)
100 g (3½ oz) rocket (arugula)
    leaves, torn
200 g (7 oz/¾ cup)
    Greek-style yoghurt
3 garlic cloves, finely chopped
4 tablespoons olive oil

Halve the eggplants lengthways and put them, skin side down, on a hot barbecue until their skins blacken, then turn and cook the cut sides for 3–4 minutes. This will give the eggplant a lovely smoky flavour. (You could roast the eggplant at 200°C/400°F for 30 minutes, though you won't get the same smoky flavour.)

Place the eggplant halves, cut side up, on serving plates. Scatter the rocket leaves over.

Combine the yoghurt, garlic and olive oil in a bowl and spoon the mixture over the eggplant and rocket leaves. Season with salt and freshly ground black pepper.

NOTE
To make this as a salad in a bowl, leave the eggplants whole and roast on a hot barbecue until their skins blacken. Once the eggplants are cool enough to handle, peel the skins off and discard. Tear the flesh into chunks and put in a bowl with the rocket leaves. Season with salt and freshly ground black pepper. Combine the yoghurt, garlic and olive oil in a small bowl. Add to the salad, toss gently and serve.

Based on the classic Egyptian breakfast dish of dukkah and eggs, this salad is one of the most popular at Kepos Street Kitchen.

HOT SMOKED SALMON & POTATO SALAD

SERVES 4

400 g (14 oz) kipfler potatoes,
    peeled, boiled and chopped
500 g (1 lb 2 oz) hot smoked salmon
    (available from fish markets
    or vacuum-packed at
    supermarkets), flaked
12 Sicilian olives, pitted
    and chopped
4 eggs, soft-boiled
3 tablespoons extra virgin olive oil
4 tablespoons hazelnut dukkah
    (see page 212) or za'atar
    (see page 214)
1 handful flat-leaf (Italian) parsley,
    leaves chopped
juice of 1 lemon
zest of ½ lemon

Put the potato, half of the salmon and the olives in a large bowl and mix gently. Tear apart 2 of the eggs and toss through the salad.

Put the olive oil, dukkah, parsley, lemon juice and zest in a bowl and whisk to combine. Pour over the salad and mix gently until combined.

To serve, tear apart the remaining 2 eggs and scatter over the salad with the remaining salmon.

Our classic green salad works with just about everything.

GREEN LEAF SALAD

SERVES 4–6 AS A SIDE DISH

2 baby cos lettuces, washed
    and leaves torn
1 avocado, cut into chunks
2 celery stalks, thinly sliced
3 spring onions (scallions),
    thinly sliced
1 Lebanese (short) cucumber,
    peeled and sliced into
    thick chunks
good-quality olive oil, to drizzle
white balsamic vinegar, to drizzle

Put the lettuce, avocado, celery, spring onion and cucumber in a large bowl and toss to combine.

Drizzle over the olive oil and balsamic vinegar according to your taste. Season with salt and freshly ground black pepper and toss using a pair of tongs to make sure the salad is well coated with the dressing.

This light and smoky scorched eggplant dish is similar to the well-known baba ghanoush.

SCORCHED EGGPLANT SALAD

SERVES 4 AS A SIDE DISH

2 eggplants (aubergines)
2 tomatoes, diced
1 large handful coriander (cilantro), leaves chopped
1 small handful mint, leaves chopped
1 large handful flat-leaf (Italian) parsley, leaves chopped
½ red onion, finely diced
2 garlic cloves, crushed
juice of 2 lemons
3 tablespoons olive oil

Scorch the eggplants on an open flame or hot barbecue until the skins have blackened and the flesh is soft. When cool enough to handle, peel off the blackened skins (don't worry if there are a few black bits on the eggplant, as this will add to the flavour). Finely chop the eggplant flesh and put it into a large bowl.

Add the remaining ingredients and mix until combined. Season with salt and freshly ground black pepper to taste. Serve.

This clean, light salad is one of the most basic in Israeli cuisine, and can become a meal in itself when you add a protein such as tuna or chicken.

ISRAELI CHOPPED VEGETABLE SALAD

SERVES 4–6 AS A SIDE DISH

3 large truss tomatoes, diced
2 Lebanese (short)
    cucumbers, diced
1 small red onion, diced
4 radishes, diced
1 handful mint, leaves chopped
2 large handfuls flat-leaf (Italian)
    parsley, leaves finely chopped
3–4 spring onions (scallions),
    finely chopped
juice of 1 lemon
125 ml (4 fl oz/½ cup) extra virgin
    olive oil

Put all of the ingredients in a large bowl, season with salt and freshly ground black pepper, and mix until combined.

If you are making this salad ahead of time, omit the lemon juice, oil and salt and pepper until you are ready to serve it.

NOTE
This salad is also delicious served with a yoghurt dressing, made by combining 250 g (9 oz) Greek-style yoghurt, 15 g (½ oz/¼ cup) chopped mint leaves, 4 crushed garlic cloves and 2 tablespoons olive oil.

I just love this salad because it works well with fish or meat,
but it's great as a vegetarian salad, too.

ZUCCHINI & PEARL BARLEY SALAD

SERVES 6–8 AS A SIDE DISH

100 g (3½ oz/½ cup) pearl barley
1 tablespoon olive oil
500 g (1 lb 2 oz) or 3 large zucchini
    (courgettes), coarsely grated
4 large handfuls flat-leaf (Italian)
    parsley, leaves finely chopped
1 large handful mint, leaves finely
    chopped, plus extra whole
    mint leaves, to garnish
3–4 spring onions (scallions),
    finely chopped
50 g (1¾ oz) chermoula
    (see page 220)

Put the pearl barley in a medium saucepan and cover with water. Place over high heat and bring to the boil. Reduce the heat to medium–high and cook for 15 minutes, or until tender. Drain the pearl barley then spread it out on a baking tray. Refrigerate until cool.

Heat the olive oil in a shallow frying pan over medium–high heat (not too high, or you will burn the zucchini, but not too low, either). Cook the zucchini in small batches until crisp and golden brown. Drain on paper towel.

Put the pearl barley and zucchini in a large bowl with the parsley, chopped mint, spring onion and chermoula. Mix well to combine and season with salt to taste. Garnish with mint leaves and serve.

Although this herb salad is a well-known basic in Mediterranean cuisine, I like to make a naughty version with chopped fried eggplant added for an extra flavour dimension.

TABOULEH

SERVES 4 AS A SIDE DISH

1 tablespoon burghul (bulgur)
4 large handfuls flat-leaf (Italian)
   parsley, leaves finely chopped
1 handful mint, leaves
   finely chopped
4 spring onions (scallions), chopped
2 tomatoes, seeds removed,
   chopped
1 Lebanese (short) cucumber,
   chopped
4 tablespoons olive oil
4 tablespoons lemon juice
pomegranate seeds, to garnish

Soak the burghul in hot water for 1 minute. Drain and squeeze out any remaining liquid. Transfer to a large bowl and set aside to cool.

Add the parsley, mint, spring onion, tomato and cucumber to the bowl with the burghul. Stir gently to combine. Stir in the olive oil and lemon juice, and season with salt and freshly ground black pepper to taste. Scatter with pomegranate seeds to serve.

Gourmet up your olives with this recipe – a perfect nibble food when you have guests over, or you can serve it with grilled fish or steak. There is enough salt in the anchovies and olives to make it unnecessary to add more.

GREEN OLIVES, WHITE ANCHOVIES & CORIANDER SEEDS

SERVES 4 AS A SIDE DISH

1 tablespoon coriander seeds

300 g (10½ oz) large green olives, pitted

1 handful coriander (cilantro), leaves finely chopped

4 tablespoons extra virgin olive oil, plus extra, to drizzle

50 g (1¾ oz) white anchovy fillets, in oil

Heat a frying pan over medium heat. Add the coriander seeds and dry-fry for 3 minutes, or until fragrant. Crush the seeds using a mortar and pestle.

Put the olives, coriander seeds, chopped coriander and olive oil in a large bowl and toss to combine. Scatter the anchovy fillets over the top and drizzle with olive oil.

Tom, who is Kristy's younger brother, is a great cook. He made this salad for us many years ago when we visited him in Melbourne and we just loved the combination of the crisp fennel and the creamy feta. It has become a favourite salad in our house as well.

TOM'S FENNEL SALAD

SERVES 4–6

*2 fennel bulbs, thinly shaved
    using a mandolin
2 Lebanese (short) cucumbers,
    thinly shaved lengthways using
    a mandolin
1 handful dill, coarsely chopped
2 large handfuls flat-leaf
    (Italian) parsley, leaves
    coarsely chopped
1 handful mint leaves
100 g (3½ oz) feta cheese, crumbled
juice of 2 lemons
3 tablespoons extra virgin olive oil
50 g (1¾ oz/⅓ cup) pine
    nuts, toasted*

Put the fennel, cucumber, dill, parsley and mint in a large bowl and toss gently to combine. Add the feta cheese and gently toss through using your hands.

Put the lemon juice and olive oil in a small bowl and whisk to combine. Pour the dressing over the salad, season with salt (with care, as the feta is quite salty) and gently mix through using your hands. Scatter the pine nuts over the top.

NOTE
If you are serving this salad with fish, use the lemon juice in the dressing, but if serving with meat you can use 1½ tablespoons white balsamic vinegar instead.

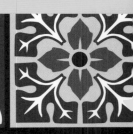

CHAPTER FIVE

DISHES FOR SHARING

THE MEDITERRANEAN WAY OF EATING IS ALL ABOUT SHARING – EVERYONE FILLING THEIR PLATES WITH FOOD FROM THE CENTRE OF THE TABLE.

A sharing table is about conversation and community. It is where ideas and opinions, as well as recipes and food, are shared. It never worried Mum if people dropped in for dinner unexpectedly, because she always had more ingredients on hand to add to the spread. Which is why I love sharing food so much, and why I don't worry when extra people turn up for a meal. A slow-cooked lamb shoulder for six can easily become a meal for ten with the addition of more salads, vegetables and dips.

Slow-roasting meat is meant to be easy, and this recipe proves that it can be. All you need to do is combine the ingredients, cover the lamb, put it in the oven and let the magic happen.

8-HOUR SLOW-ROASTED LAMB SHOULDER

SERVES 4-6

2 tablespoons coriander seeds,
    lightly toasted
100 ml (3½ fl oz) olive oil
1 tablespoon sea salt flakes
½ tablespoon freshly ground
    black pepper
1 lamb shoulder, bone in, about
    2 kg (4 lb 8 oz)
1 garlic bulb, cut in half crossways

Preheat the oven to 180°C (350°F).

Use a mortar and pestle to lightly bruise the toasted coriander seeds. Transfer to a small bowl and add the olive oil, salt and pepper. Combine and rub the mixture over the lamb shoulder.

Put the lamb in a roasting tin with the garlic. Cover the lamb with baking paper. Wrap a layer of foil tightly over the lamb and the edge of the roasting tin so that no steam can escape during cooking and the lamb cooks in its own juices. Cook for 2 hours. Reduce the temperature to 120°C (235°F) and cook for a further 6 hours.

The meat is cooked when it pulls away from the bone easily. At this point, increase the oven temperature to 200°C (400°F). Remove the foil and baking paper and cook the meat for a further 10 minutes to crisp up and colour the outside of the lamb.

Serve the lamb with any or all of the dishes in the big banquet on page 132.

Classic dishes that aren't Middle Eastern always present a challenge for me as a chef – I love to see how I can add my own stamp. The saffron and coriander are not normally expected with battered fish, and the sumac aïoli is another delicious twist.

BATTERED FISH WITH SUMAC AÏOLI

SERVES 6

300 ml (10½ fl oz) soda water (club soda)
2 teaspoons salt
150 g (5½ oz/1 cup) self-raising flour, sifted
pinch of saffron threads, soaked in 2 tablespoons hot water
1 tablespoon crushed coriander seeds
2 litres (70 fl oz/8 cups) vegetable oil or rice bran oil, for frying
80 g (2¾ oz) cornflour (cornstarch)
600 g (1 lb 5 oz) firm white fish (such as flathead, barramundi or monkfish), cut into finger-sized strips (goujons)
potato chips (fries), to serve
sumac aïoli (see page 226), to serve

Put the soda water and salt in a large bowl and combine. Slowly fold in the flour to make a smooth batter. Add the saffron and its soaking water and the coriander seeds. Mix through and set aside.

Put the vegetable oil in a large deep saucepan over high heat. To test if the oil is hot enough, drop in a small amount of batter. When it starts to sizzle, the oil is ready for deep-frying.

Put the cornflour in a shallow bowl. Lightly dust the fish goujons in the cornflour, dip into the batter and cook, a few at a time, for 3–5 minutes, or until golden brown. (Don't overcrowd the pan, as this will reduce the temperature of the oil.) Drain on paper towel.

Serve the fish with chips and sumac aïoli.

Meatloaf fans will love this delicious layered variation on the traditional theme. I pre-cook the potatoes so the meat doesn't have to be overcooked, and you can serve the meat medium or well done, as you like it.

KEFTA SENIEH (BAKED KEFTA)

SERVES 6–8

700 g (1 lb 9 oz) desiree (all-purpose) potatoes, peeled and cut into 1 cm (½ inch) slices

1 kg (2 lb 4 oz) coarsely minced (ground) lamb

1 teaspoon ground coriander

2 teaspoons ground cumin

1 teaspoon chilli flakes

4 tablespoons olive oil

2 large handfuls flat-leaf (Italian) parsley, leaves finely chopped, plus coarsely chopped leaves, extra, to garnish

1 small brown onion, finely chopped

2 teaspoons sea salt flakes

butter or olive oil, for greasing

4 tomatoes, thickly sliced

1 red onion, thickly sliced

400 g (10 oz) tin chopped tomatoes

2 tablespoons mild paprika

chopped coriander (cilantro) leaves, to garnish

Preheat the oven to 180°C (350°F).

Put the potato slices in a large saucepan and cover with cold water. Cook over medium heat until firm, about 10 minutes. Drain and set aside.

Put the lamb mince, ground coriander, cumin, chilli flakes, olive oil, chopped parsley, onion and salt in a large bowl and mix by hand to combine. Roll the mince mixture into sausage shapes, about 60 g (2¼ oz) each, then flatten with your hands. (This shape helps the keftas sit upright when layering with the potato, tomato and onion.)

Grease a baking dish with butter (this will give a richer flavour to the dish) or olive oil. Layer the lamb kefta with the potato, tomato and red onion slices horizontally across the baking dish until all are used (see picture, right). Scatter any remaining onion rings over the top.

Put the tinned tomatoes and paprika in a small bowl. Mix and season with salt and freshly ground black pepper. Spoon this mixture over the layered kefta.

Cook in the oven for 40 minutes. Increase the temperature to 200°C (400°F) and cook for a further 15 minutes. (This will give the dish a nice colour.) Pour off a little of the cooking liquid. Scatter with chopped parsley and coriander and serve in bowls.

To work out how long to cook a whole fish in the oven, I allow three minutes per 100 g (3½ oz). So an 800 g (1 lb 12 oz) whole fish will require 24 minutes baking time.

BAKED WHOLE SNAPPER WITH WALNUTS, CHILLI & TAHINI DRESSING

SERVES 4

700–800 g (1 lb 9 oz–1 lb 12 oz) whole snapper, cleaned
4 tablespoons olive oil, plus 2 tablespoons extra
120 g (4¼ oz) walnuts, coarsely chopped
1 long green chilli, coarsely chopped (seeds optional)
1 teaspoon ground coriander
1 teaspoon ground cumin
2 large handfuls flat-leaf (Italian) parsley, leaves chopped
pinch of sea salt
4 tablespoons tahini dressing (see page 232)

Preheat the oven to 180°C (350°F).

Score the snapper on the diagonal 2–3 times on each side. Put on a baking tray lined with baking paper.

Put the 4 tablespoons of olive oil in a medium frying pan over medium heat. Add the walnuts and chilli and cook until lightly toasted. Add the coriander and cumin, stir and remove from the heat. Mix through the parsley, extra olive oil and salt.

Spread the walnut mixture over the snapper. Cook in the oven for 21–24 minutes, depending on the size of the fish. Serve on a platter with the tahini dressing on the side to spoon over.

A Moroccan festive dish, bastilla combines the sweet and the salty. It's not unusual to see cinnamon used with meat and other savoury dishes in Mediterranean cooking, and it works really well in this savoury pie, where it's used to add sweetness along with the icing sugar that is sprinkled on top. For a special occasion, cut out a stencil and dust with the icing sugar to create a pattern.

CHICKEN BASTILLA

SERVES 6-8

65 g (2¼ oz/½ cup) slivered almonds

70 g (2½ oz/½ cup) pistachio
    nut kernels

3 tablespoons olive oil

1 brown onion, finely chopped

2 garlic cloves, finely chopped

1 teaspoon ground cinnamon, plus
    extra, for sprinkling

1 teaspoon finely grated ginger

2 teaspoons ground cumin

2 teaspoons ground coriander

2 teaspoons fennel seeds

4 boneless, skinless chicken
    breasts (about 600 g/1 lb 5 oz),
    minced (ground)

pinch of saffron threads, soaked in
    2 tablespoons hot water

1 egg, lightly beaten

1 handful coriander (cilantro)
    leaves, coarsely chopped

120 g (4¼ oz) butter, melted

15 sheets (about 300 g/10½ oz)
    filo pastry

icing (confectioners') sugar,
    for sprinkling

Preheat the oven to 220°C (425°F). Put the almonds and pistachios on a baking tray and toast in the oven for 5 minutes, or until the almonds get a bit of colour. Transfer the nuts to a food processor (leave the oven on) and pulse until coarsely ground. Set aside.

Heat the olive oil in a large frying pan over medium–high heat. Add the onion and garlic and cook for 3–4 minutes. Add the cinnamon, ginger, cumin, coriander and fennel seeds and cook for 1 minute. Add the chicken and cook for 5 minutes. Remove the pan from the heat and stir through the saffron and its soaking water. Set aside to cool.

Season the cooled chicken mixture with salt and freshly ground black pepper. Add the beaten egg and chopped coriander. Mix to combine.

Grease a round 24 cm (9½ inch) cake tin with butter. Lay a sheet of filo pastry in the tin; the sheets will hang over the edge. Brush with melted butter and scatter over a thin layer of the nut mixture. Add the next layer of filo in the opposite direction (you are going to fold all of these layers over to seal the pie). Repeat with the filo, butter and nuts until you have used all but 1 sheet of the filo.

Spoon the chicken mixture on top of the layered filo. Press down the chicken evenly. Bring each filo layer onto the top of the pie, closing it up, adding the melted butter and nuts for each layer as you do.

Bake the bastilla for 20 minutes. Reduce the oven temperature to 180°C (350°F). Take the pie out of the oven and flip it out onto a baking tray. Cook for a further 10 minutes or until it has a good colour on all sides. Serve sprinkled with icing sugar and cinnamon.

Kristy is the queen of roast chicken and potatoes. Hers is always better than mine, which is why I am giving you her recipe.

SUNDAY NIGHT ROAST CHICKEN

SERVES 4-6

1 whole 1.2–1.4 kg (2 lb
    10 oz–3 lb 2 oz) chicken
1 tablespoon hazelnut dukkah
    (see page 212)
4 tablespoons olive oil, plus extra
    for greasing
1 lemon
green leaf salad (see page 106),
    to serve

POTATOES

750 g (1 lb 10 oz) desiree
    (all-purpose) potatoes, peeled
    and chopped into chunks
125 ml (4 fl oz/½ cup) olive oil
1 teaspoon sea salt

Preheat the oven to 200°C (400°F). Line a roasting tin with foil and then baking paper. Place a wire rack on top. Rinse the cavity of the chicken with cold water and pat dry with paper towel. Set aside.

Combine the dukkah and olive oil in a small bowl. Take the chicken and carefully separate the skin from the breast and drumsticks with your fingers. Using your hands, take some of the dukkah mixture and spread it under the skin of the chicken breast and drumsticks.

Peel the rind from the lemon and set aside. Cut the lemon in half and put the halves inside the chicken. Season the chicken with salt and freshly ground black pepper and rub the skin well with extra olive oil.

Put the chicken, breast side down, on the rack in the roasting tin and cook for 20 minutes. Turn the chicken over, add a roasting tin for the potatoes (see below), reduce the temperature to 180°C (350°F) and cook for 40 minutes. The chicken is cooked when you prick the side near the drumstick and the juices run clear.

Meanwhile, cover the potatoes with cold water in a large saucepan over high heat. Bring to the boil and par-cook for 10 minutes, or until soft enough for a fork to go through. Just before the potatoes are ready to be drained, put the olive oil in the heated roasting tin and return to the oven. Drain the potatoes in a colander and allow the steam to be released. Once the potatoes have cooled a little, gently move them around in the colander to roughen up the surface. Take the roasting tin out of the oven at the same time you are turning the chicken in its roasting tin. Put the potatoes, lemon rind and salt in the roasting tin and toss in the hot oil. Cook for 40–45 minutes, until golden brown.

Carve the chicken and serve with the potatoes and a salad.

I have earned lots of brownie points from my nieces and nephews for serving up these meatballs. Eaten with rice or tossed through pasta, they are packed with vegetables and protein – and they're delicious.

CHICKEN MEATBALLS WITH SILVERBEET & TOMATO

SERVES 8-10

1 kg (2 lb 4 oz) minced (ground) chicken
1 large handful coriander (cilantro), leaves chopped
100 g (3½ oz) fresh or dry breadcrumbs
3 eggs
3 tablespoons extra virgin olive oil
½ teaspoon freshly ground black pepper
1½ tablespoons sea salt
4 tablespoons olive oil
1 large brown onion, finely chopped
5 garlic cloves, diced
2 large red chillies, chopped (optional)
2 x 400 g (14 oz) tins crushed tomatoes
500 ml (17 fl oz/2 cups) chicken stock
200 g (7 oz) silverbeet (Swiss chard) leaves, coarsely chopped
rice or pasta, to serve

Put the chicken mince in a large bowl with the coriander, breadcrumbs, eggs, extra virgin olive oil, pepper and salt. Mix to combine, then form the mixture into golf-ball sized balls.

Heat the olive oil in a large saucepan over medium–high heat. Cook the chicken balls until just golden brown in three batches. (They will cook all the way through in the tomato sauce in the next step.) Transfer the chicken balls to a bowl and set aside.

Add the onion, garlic and chilli, if using, to the saucepan and cook over medium heat for 5 minutes, until softened. Add the tomatoes and stock and bring to the boil. Return the browned chicken balls to the saucepan and cook for 35–40 minutes over medium heat.

Add the silverbeet in three batches, allowing the leaves to steam with the lid on and shrink down after each addition. Season with salt and freshly ground black pepper to taste and cook for a further 5 minutes, or until the silverbeet has wilted into the sauce.

Serve with rice or pasta of your choice.

Barbounia, also known as red mullet, is a small fish that is very popular in the Mediterranean. It is the equivalent of whitebait, so you eat it whole – head, body and tail.

CRISPY BARBOUNIA WITH TOMATO SALSA & HARISSA

SERVES 4 AS A MAIN OR 8 AS PART OF A MEZZE DINNER

150 g (5½ oz/1 cup) plain (all-purpose) flour
½ teaspoon ground chilli
1 tablespoon mild sweet paprika
½ teaspoon ground cumin
½ teaspoon salt
1 litre (35 fl oz/4 cups) vegetable oil, for frying
1 kg (2 lb 4 oz) barbounia (baby red mullet)

SALSA
3 large truss tomatoes
3 tablespoons red harissa (see page 222)
1 small handful mint, leaves finely chopped

Put the flour, chilli, paprika, cumin and salt in a large bowl. Mix to combine.

Put the vegetable oil in a large saucepan over high heat. Heat to 170°C (325°F), or until a cube of bread dropped into it turns golden brown in 20 seconds.

Dust the fish on both sides with the flour mixture, until well coated.

Deep-fry the fish in the oil, a few pieces at a time, for 3–4 minutes. Do not overcrowd the saucepan with fish, as it will cause the oil temperature to drop. Drain the fish on paper towel.

To make the salsa, grate the tomatoes into a medium bowl. Add the harissa and mint, toss to combine and season with salt and freshly ground black pepper to taste.

Serve the fish on a platter with the salsa in a bowl on the side.

In our take on the classic spinach pie, we've added lots of herbs, spring onions and lemon zest for a tasty fresh and herby flavour.

FETA, FILO & SILVERBEET PIE

SERVES 6-8

3 tablespoons olive oil
1 onion, finely chopped
2 garlic cloves, crushed
1 kg (2 lb 4 oz) silverbeet (Swiss chard), white and green parts thoroughly washed and coarsely chopped
1 large handful mint, leaves coarsely chopped
1 small handful dill, coarsely chopped
1 large handful flat-leaf (Italian) parsley, leaves coarsely chopped
4–6 spring onions (scallions), all the white and half the green parts finely chopped
zest of 1 lemon
200 g (7 oz) feta cheese, crumbled
250 g (9 oz) smooth ricotta
2 eggs, beaten
130 g (4½ oz) butter, melted
20 sheets (about 360 g/12¾ oz) filo pastry

Preheat the oven to 170°C (325°F). Heat the olive oil in a small frying pan over medium heat. Add the onion and garlic and cook for 2–3 minutes, without colouring. Set aside.

Wilt the silverbeet in batches in a large saucepan with a lid over high heat, stirring with a pair of tongs occasionally. There should be enough moisture on the leaves after washing them to help the wilting process, which should take about 7 minutes. Transfer each batch to a colander to drain and cool.

Squeeze the cooled silverbeet with your hands several times until the excess liquid has been removed – you'll be surprised by how much there is. Transfer the squeezed silverbeet to a large bowl.

Add the mint, dill, parsley, spring onion, lemon zest, feta, ricotta and beaten egg to the bowl with the silverbeet and combine. Season with salt and freshly ground black pepper, keeping in mind the feta is salty.

Place a sheet of filo in a large baking dish and brush with the melted butter; it may overhang. Repeat, brushing each sheet with butter and laying it on top of the others, until you have used 17 of the filo sheets.

Spoon the silverbeet and cheese mixture evenly on top of the layered filo pastry sheets. Gently scrunch up one of the remaining filo sheets so it forms gentle folds and put it on top of the filling. Brush with melted butter and repeat with the remaining 2 sheets of filo. Bring in the ends of the overhanging filo sheets and fold onto the top of the pie. Brush the edges with any remaining butter and bake for 45–50 minutes, or until golden brown.

Blue eye cod and monkfish are my favourite types of fish to use for these kefta, and I'll usually serve them with scorched eggplant (see page 107), a drizzle of good-quality olive oil and pomegranate molasses (see page 229), and a scattering of pomegranate seeds and mint leaves.

FISH KEFTA

SERVES 6

1 kg (2 lb 4 oz) firm white fish
2 large handfuls flat-leaf (Italian) parsley, finely chopped
80 g (2¾ oz / ½ cup) pine nuts
1 teaspoon sea salt
3 tablespoons olive oil, plus extra for frying
mint leaves and pomegranate seeds, to garnish
lemon halves, to serve

Mince the fish to a coarse consistency. (To do this, use a mincer on the coarse setting or pulse in a food processor. You can also dice the fish with a knife, then mince using a mezzaluna.)

Put the minced fish in a large bowl and add the parsley, pine nuts, salt and oil. Combine well and divide the mixture into 18 portions, and mould each portion into a sausage-shaped kefta.

Preheat the oven to 180°C (350°F).

Heat a little extra olive oil in an ovenproof frying pan over medium heat. In batches, cook the kefta on one side until golden, then turn the kefta and put the frying pan in the oven to cook for 3 minutes. (Ideally, you could use two frying pans at the same time, cooking on the stovetop while the other is in the oven.) You could also cook these kefta on a barbecue.

Scatter over mint leaves and pomegranate seeds, and serve with lemon halves.

BIG BANQUET

Designed to impress with the many complex flavours and textures, this banquet is ideal for celebrating a special occasion – birthdays, anniversaries, christenings, anything ...

1 **8-HOUR SLOW-ROASTED LAMB SHOULDER** see page 118

2 **CAULIFLOWER & CRANBERRY SALAD** see page 91

3 **WARM MOROCCAN CARROT SALAD** see page 87

4 **CHICKEN BASTILLA** see page 124

5 **BEETROOT PICKLED CUCUMBERS** see page 217

6 **GREEN OLIVES, WHITE ANCHOVIES & CORIANDER SEEDS** see page 113

As a child, I never liked okra, but now I can't get enough of it – it's one of those vegetables that seems to grow on you. This recipe is a favourite of mine as it combines two perfect ingredients – okra and lamb. The slow cooking of the lamb releases beautiful juices that the okra braises in and soaks up. This dish is a great one for a weekend when you have time to potter around while it works its magic. Serve it with rice to soak up the delicious sauce.

BRAISED HARISSA LAMB SHOULDER WITH OKRA

SERVES 8

125 g (4½ oz/½ cup) red harissa
    (see page 222)
6 garlic cloves, chopped
1 large chilli, finely diced
125 ml (4 fl oz/½ cup) olive oil,
    plus 4 tablespoons extra
2 x 400 g (14 oz) tins
    crushed tomatoes
100 ml (3½ fl oz) vegetable stock
1 lamb shoulder, bone in, about
    2 kg (4 lb 8 oz)
300 g (10½ oz) okra
1 large handful coriander (cilantro),
    leaves picked

Preheat the oven to 170°C (325°F). Put the harissa, garlic, chilli, 125 ml olive oil, tomato and stock in a large bowl. Season with salt and freshly ground black pepper. Mix to combine.

Put the lamb shoulder in a large roasting tin. Pour the harissa mixture over and massage it well into the lamb. Leave the excess liquid in the roasting tin. Cover the lamb and roasting tin with a sheet of baking paper then with foil, wrapping and sealing it tightly so no steam will escape. Cook the lamb in the preheated oven. (It will need to cook for a total of 4½ hours.)

When the lamb has been in the oven for 3½ hours, prepare the okra. Trim the okra heads but don't cut them all the way off so the okra will hold its shape while cooking. Wash the okra in a colander then drain off any excess liquid. Lay the okra on a clean dry tea towel (dish towel) and rub until they are completely dry.

Heat the olive oil in a medium frying pan over medium–high heat. Cook the okra until it is a nice golden colour. Set aside.

At the 4-hour mark, remove the roasting tin from the oven and remove the foil and baking paper. Spoon the okra over the lamb and cook for a further 30 minutes, uncovered. Check there is still some liquid in the tin and add water if necessary to maintain the juiciness of the lamb and to make a sauce. The lamb is ready when it can be easily pulled apart with a fork or tongs. Serve with the sauce and scatter over the coriander.

Warming, comforting and just like the stew my mum made when I was growing up. Serve it with couscous like she did for an even more hearty meal.

LAMB & CHICKPEA STEW

SERVES 6-8

170 ml (5½ fl oz/⅔ cup) olive oil
1 kg (2 lb 4 oz) lamb shanks
2 litres (70 fl oz/8 cups) good-quality vegetable stock
2 small brown onions, coarsely chopped
3 garlic cloves
3 celery stalks, coarsely chopped
2 red chillies, finely chopped
1 tablespoon ground turmeric
2 tablespoons coriander seeds
2 tablespoons cumin seeds
400 g (14 oz) tin chickpeas, drained
1 litre (35 fl oz/4 cups) stock reserved from cooking the lamb shanks
1 handful coriander (cilantro), leaves picked

Heat 4 tablespoons of the olive oil in a large saucepan over medium heat. Sear the lamb shanks on each side until well coloured. Add the vegetable stock and bring to the boil. Reduce to a simmer, cover with a lid and cook for 3 hours, or until the shank meat falls off the bone, skimming the surface from time to time. Set aside to cool a little.

When the lamb shanks are cool enough to handle, take the meat off them and break it into big chunks. Reserve the stock.

Put the remaining olive oil in a large saucepan over medium heat. Cook the onion and garlic for 5 minutes, or until softened. Add the celery and chilli and cook for 3–4 minutes. Add the turmeric and coriander and cumin seeds and cook for 2 minutes. Add the chickpeas and the reserved lamb shank stock and cook for 25 minutes. Season with sea salt to taste.

Add the shredded lamb to the chickpea stew and cook over low heat for 10 minutes.

To serve, ladle the stew into large bowls and garnish with the coriander leaves.

Mujaddara – which translates as 'jewelled rice' – works really well on its own or with a protein dish. When Mum had cooked the mujaddara and was preparing the rest of dinner, we kids would sneak into the kitchen, take a big spoonful and add a dollop of yoghurt for a snack. It's also a great vegetarian dish with salads.

LENTIL RICE (MUJADDARA)

SERVES 6-8 AS A SIDE DISH

215 g (7½ oz/1 cup) green lentils
3 tablespoons olive oil, plus 125 ml
    (4 fl oz/½ cup) olive oil, extra
400 g (14 oz/2 cups) basmati or
    jasmine rice
1 tablespoon ground cumin
1 teaspoon sea salt
750 ml (26 fl oz/3 cups)
    boiling water
2 brown onions, thinly sliced
1 handful flat-leaf (Italian) parsley,
    leaves chopped
100 g (3½ oz/⅔ cup) pine
    nuts, toasted

Put the lentils and 1.25 litres (44 fl oz/5 cups) cold water in a large saucepan over medium heat. Bring to the boil then reduce the heat to a gentle simmer for 18 minutes, or until the lentils are soft but not mushy. Drain and set aside.

Heat the 3 tablespoons of olive oil in a medium saucepan over medium heat. Add the rice and toss lightly until it warms through. Add the cumin and salt and mix through. Add the boiling water and bring to the boil. Cover the saucepan with a lid, reduce the heat to low and cook for 18 minutes. Remove the saucepan from the heat and let the rice rest for 5 minutes with the lid on. Remove the lid and fluff the rice with a fork.

Put the 125 ml of oil in a frying pan over medium–high heat. Cook the onion until golden brown and slightly crispy, taking care not to overcook it.

Put the lentils, rice, onion, parsley and pine nuts in a large bowl and gently fold with a fork to combine.

The flavours here are different from traditional osso buco, and I don't flour the osso buco before browning them, which many people do. I agree you get a much nicer colour if you flour the osso buco, but reducing the sauce through the cooking process gives it a more intense and natural flavour.

OSSO BUCO WITH JERUSALEM ARTICHOKES & CORIANDER GREMOLATA

SERVES 4

2 tablespoons olive oil
1.2 kg (2 lb 10 oz) veal osso buco
1 small onion, coarsely chopped
3 garlic cloves, coarsely chopped
1 celery stalk, coarsely chopped
400 g (14 oz) tin crushed tomatoes
250 ml (9 fl oz/1 cup) beef stock
500 g (1 lb 2 oz) jerusalem
  artichokes, washed and peeled
coriander gremolata (see page 232)

Preheat the oven to 180°C (350°F).

Heat the olive oil in a large braising pan or large deep ovenproof frying pan with a lid over medium heat. Brown the osso buco on each side. Remove the osso buco to a plate and set aside.

To the same pan, add the onion, garlic and celery and cook for 5 minutes, or until soft. Add the tomato and stock and stir to combine. Return the osso buco to the pan. Season with salt and freshly ground black pepper, but do not add too much as the flavour will intensify as the sauce reduces. Bring to the boil, cover with the lid and transfer the pan to the oven. Cook for 3 hours.

After 3 hours, add the jerusalem artichokes, cover and cook for a further 1 hour, or until the meat falls off the bone.

Add additional seasoning if needed, and serve with the coriander gremolata.

Not your predictable risotto, this eggplant version is full of flavour and a favourite with vegetarians or as a side dish with meat.

PERSIAN EGGPLANT RISOTTO

SERVES 4-6

4 tablespoons olive oil
1 onion, diced
4 garlic cloves, crushed
1 litre (35 fl oz/4 cups)
    vegetable stock
360 g (12 oz/1¾ cups) arborio
    or carnaroli rice
250 ml (9 fl oz/1 cup) dry white wine
2½ cups Persian eggplant
    (see page 95)
1 tablespoon butter, at
    room temperature
1 small handful coriander (cilantro),
    leaves chopped

Heat the olive oil in a large frying pan over medium–low heat for 1 minute. Cook the onion and garlic for 4–5 minutes, stirring occasionally, without letting them colour.

Meanwhile, put the stock in a large saucepan over high heat. Bring to the boil, reduce the heat to low and simmer until ready to use.

Add the rice to the frying pan and mix well. Cook for 2–3 minutes, stirring occasionally. Pour in the wine and cook, uncovered, until the rice has absorbed all the liquid and the alcohol has evaporated, stirring frequently.

Add the Persian eggplant to the frying pan and stir well. Add the stock, a ladle at a time, stirring occasionally until all the stock has been added. This should take about 20 minutes, and the rice should still be slightly firm. Add salt to taste and gently stir through the butter. Scatter over the coriander and serve immediately.

Chreime is a North African-Jewish fish stew that's delicious with sweet bread such as challah or brioche to dip into the spicy, tomatoey sauce. I like to use barramundi for this, as the earthiness works well with the spices, but you can use any white-fleshed fish.

ROY'S CHREIME (FISH STEW)

SERVES 6

3 tablespoons olive oil

2 large red capsicums (peppers), seeds removed and cut into strips

8 garlic cloves, coarsely chopped

1 green chilli, chopped (seeds optional)

3 ripe tomatoes, diced

2 tablespoons smoked paprika

2 teaspoons ground cumin

400 ml (14 fl oz) fish stock

6 white-fleshed fish fillets (about 1.2 kg/2 lb 8 oz)

1 large handful coriander (cilantro), leaves coarsely chopped

Heat the olive oil in a deep frying pan with a lid over medium heat. Cook the capsicum and garlic for 5 minutes, or until fragrant and slightly softened. Add the chilli and cook for 1 minute. Add the tomato and cook for 5 minutes. Add the paprika and cumin, stir and cook for another 2 minutes. Add the fish stock, reduce the heat to medium–low and cook for 15 minutes. Check the seasoning and adjust with salt if necessary.

Add the fish to the stew, skin side up. Cover the frying pan and cook over medium–low heat for 10 minutes. Remove the lid and let the sauce simmer for 5 minutes. Increase or decrease this cooking time by 2–4 minutes according to the size of the fish fillets. Add the coriander and serve at the table from the frying pan.

This is such an easy dish to make and has such a fantastic festive look and feel to it. What I like about this dish now, being an Australian, is the idea of a traditional roast lamb for Sunday lunch with Middle Eastern flavours.

APRICOT & NUT-STUFFED LEG OF LAMB

SERVES 6

1.5–2 kg (3 lb 5 oz–4 lb 8 oz) leg of lamb, deboned and butterflied
4 tablespoons olive oil

STUFFING
40 g (1½ oz) fresh (⅔ cup) or dry (⅓ cup) breadcrumbs
50 g (1¾ oz/⅓ cup) pine nuts, toasted
50 g (1¾ oz) pistachio nut kernels, lightly crushed
100 g (3½ oz/¾ cup) coarsely chopped dried apricots
zest of 1 lemon
2 garlic cloves, crushed
1 handful flat-leaf (Italian) parsley, leaves finely chopped
½ teaspoon ground cumin

Preheat the oven to 180°C (350°F). Bring the lamb to room temperature.

To make the stuffing, combine all the ingredients in a large bowl.

Lay the lamb out on a work surface and spread the stuffing all over it. Roll up the meat lengthways and tie securely with kitchen string.

Heat the olive oil in an ovenproof frying pan or a flameproof roasting tin over high heat. Sear the lamb on all sides until coloured.

Transfer the pan or tin to the preheated oven and cook for 45–60 minutes.

Remove the lamb from the oven and let it rest, covered with foil, for 15–20 minutes. Carve and serve.

One of my mum's favourites for when guests come over, this dish is big on the wow factor and absolutely delicious, too.

STUFFED SPATCHCOCKS WITH LAMB & PINE NUTS

SERVES 8

3 tablespoons olive oil
2 brown onions, finely diced
3 garlic cloves, crushed
¼ teaspoon ground cinnamon
¼ teaspoon freshly grated nutmeg
¼ teaspoon allspice
500 g (1 lb 2 oz) minced
    (ground) lamb
50 g (1¾ oz/⅓ cup) pine
    nuts, toasted
4 x 500 g (1 lb 2 oz) spatchcocks

MARINADE
125 ml (4 fl oz/½ cup) olive oil
2 teaspoons allspice
1 tablespoon pomegranate
    molasses (see page 229)

Preheat the oven to 180°C (350°F). Line a baking tray with baking paper.

Heat the olive oil in a medium frying pan over medium heat. Add the onion and garlic and cook for 3–4 minutes. Add the cinnamon, nutmeg and allspice and cook for a further 1–2 minutes. Add the lamb mince and stir occasionally until cooked. Season with salt and freshly ground black pepper to taste. Remove from the heat, add the pine nuts and mix to combine.

Rinse the cavity of each spatchcock with cold water and pat dry with paper towel. Stuff the cavities with the mince mixture. You can push a toothpick through the cavity wall to secure it (but don't forget to remove it before serving).

To make the marinade, mix the olive oil, allspice and pomegranate molasses together and rub over the spatchcocks.

Put the spatchcocks on the prepared tray and cook for 40–45 minutes. Remove from the oven and leave to rest for 5–10 minutes.

Serve on a large platter.

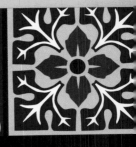
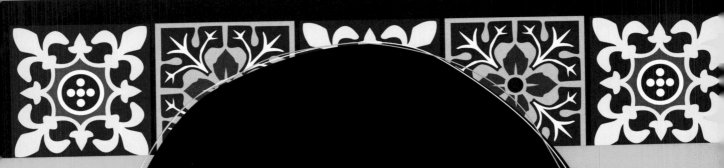

CHAPTER SIX

CAKES & DESSERTS

IN ISRAEL, THERE IS A LOVELY TRADITION OF HAVING A PLATE OF SWEET TREATS READY TO BE SHARED WHEN VISITORS DROP BY.

Everyone knows baklava, but there are plenty more delicious Middle Eastern sweet options, too. I like to create variations of these desserts, or add Middle Eastern twists to desserts from other culinary traditions. So I have merged baklava with a classic semifreddo, added cardamom to a chocolate cake, transformed the Aussie pav, and lots more.

A great dessert for a dinner party, this semifreddo can be made in advance. Serve it on its own, with caramelised figs or even a chocolate sauce.

BAKLAVA SEMIFREDDO

SERVES 6–8

160 g (5½ oz) caster
    (superfine) sugar
3 egg whites, at room temperature
500 ml (17 fl oz/2 cups) thin
    (pouring) cream
250 g (9 oz) baklava, cut into
    small pieces
zest of ½ lemon
50 g (1¾ oz) pistachio nut kernels,
    toasted and chopped

Line a 20 cm x 10 cm (8 inch x 4 inch) or similar rectangular loaf (bar) tin with plastic wrap, allowing it to overhang the sides.

Put the sugar and 4 tablespoons water in a medium saucepan over medium–high heat and bring to the boil without stirring; brush down the inside of the saucepan with a pastry brush dipped in water if there is excess sugar on the side. Continue to cook until the mixture reaches 130°C (266°F), testing with a sugar (candy) thermometer if you have one, or until firm-ball stage when the mixture starts to thicken but has no colour. This will take 10–12 minutes from the time the mixture starts to boil.

Meanwhile, use an electric mixer with a whisk attachment to whisk the egg whites until soft peaks form. When the sugar syrup has reached 130°C (266°F), slowly start to pour it over the egg whites with the mixer still going and whisk until you have a silky, thick and glossy meringue.

Put the cream in a separate bowl and whisk until soft peaks form.

Add the cream, baklava, lemon zest and pistachios to the bowl with the meringue. Fold gently to combine, taking care not to overmix.

Pour the mixture into the loaf tin and fold over the plastic wrap to cover. Freeze overnight.

To serve, turn the baklava semifreddo out onto a plate and remove the plastic wrap.

Even though it isn't a Middle Eastern slice, this classic has become a regular on the cake display at Kepos Street Kitchen. Kristy's version uses maple syrup, which adds an elegant depth of flavour.

KRISTY'S FAMOUS CARAMEL SLICE

MAKES 20 PIECES

BASE
300 g (10½ oz/2 cups) plain
    (all-purpose) flour
90 g (3¼ oz/1 cup)
    desiccated coconut
185 g (6½ oz/1 cup, lightly packed)
    dark brown sugar
250 g (9 oz) butter, melted

CARAMEL
175 g (6 oz/½ cup) maple syrup
    or golden syrup
175 g (6 oz) butter, melted
3 x 395 g (14 oz) tins sweetened
    condensed milk

CHOCOLATE TOPPING
250 g (9 oz) good-quality dark
    chocolate, coarsely chopped
4 tablespoons light olive oil

Preheat the oven to 180°C (350°F). Line a 20 cm x 30 cm (8 inch x 12 inch) cake tin with baking paper, allowing it to overhang at the ends for easy removal of the slice.

To make the base, put the flour, coconut, sugar and melted butter in a medium bowl and combine. Spread over the base of the tin and press in evenly using the back of a spoon. Bake for 15 minutes.

Meanwhile, prepare the caramel. Put the maple syrup, melted butter and sweetened condensed milk in a large heavy-based saucepan over medium–low heat and cook, stirring constantly, for 5–7 minutes, or until it starts to thicken.

When the base is cooked, pour the caramel over it and bake for 20 minutes, or until the caramel is a light golden brown. Cool the slice to room temperature and put in the fridge overnight.

When the chilled caramel is firm, make the chocolate topping. Put the chocolate in a bowl and melt in the microwave. Add the olive oil and stir until very smooth. Pour the melted chocolate over the caramel and return to the fridge for 5–10 hours, until firm.

When set, lift the slice out of the tin and cut into 20 pieces.

One of my favourite biscuits from childhood is mamoul, on which this recipe is based. I recollect that it used to take my nana forever to make mamoul, so I have created a much simpler version of it that I think tastes just as good as the original.

CHEWY PISTACHIO SLICE

MAKES 24 SMALL BARS

BASE
160 g (5½ oz) plain
  (all-purpose) flour
75 g (2½ oz/⅓ cup) caster
  (superfine) sugar
120 g (4¼ oz) cold butter,
  cut into cubes

TOPPING
4 eggs
285 g (10 oz/1½ cups, lightly
  packed) dark brown sugar
1 teaspoon natural vanilla extract
4 tablespoons plain
  (all-purpose) flour
1 teaspoon ground cinnamon
2 teaspoons baking powder
½ teaspoon salt
400 g (14 oz/4 cups) pistachio nut
  kernels, coarsely chopped
icing (confectioners') sugar, to dust

Preheat the oven to 170°C (325°F). Line a 20 cm x 30 cm (8 inch x 12 inch) baking tin with baking paper.

To make the base, put the flour, sugar and butter in a food processor and pulse until the mixture resembles breadcrumbs. Spread the mixture evenly over the base of the tin and press in lightly. Bake for 20 minutes, or until golden brown.

To make the topping, put the eggs, sugar, vanilla, flour, cinnamon, baking powder, salt and pistachios in a large bowl and combine with your hands. Spread the mixture evenly over the base and bake for 20–25 minutes, until the topping feels firm.

Cool in the tin on a wire rack, then cut into small bars and serve dusted with icing sugar.

Chocolate and cardamom is a beautiful combination, and this is a great gluten-free cake for people with wheat intolerance.

CHOCOLATE & CARDAMOM CAKE

SERVES 8–12

400 g (14 oz) dark chocolate,
    coarsely chopped
250 g (9 oz) unsalted butter
6 eggs
400 g (14 oz) caster
    (superfine) sugar
120 g (4¼ oz) almond meal
½ teaspoon ground cardamom
20 g (¾ oz) unsweetened cocoa
    powder, to dust
cream or ice cream, to serve

Preheat the oven to 180°C (350°F). Grease a 24 cm (9½ in) spring-form cake tin and line the base with baking paper.

Put the chocolate and butter in a bowl and melt in the microwave. Set aside to cool at room temperature.

Use an electric mixer with a whisk attachment to whisk the eggs and sugar until light and fluffy. Add the chocolate and fold in gently. Add the almond meal and cardamom and fold through.

Pour the mixture into the prepared tin. Bake for 40 minutes, or until the cake has a nice firm crust but is still slightly wobbly in the middle.

Cool in the tin on a wire rack. When cool, remove the spring-form ring and put the cake on a serving plate. Dust with the sifted cocoa powder.

Serve this cake at room temperature with fresh cream or ice cream, or reheat it. Store the cake in a cool place but not the fridge, as it will set and become too firm.

It may seem an unusual pairing, but dates and dukkah work well together in these brownies to create a salty and sweet taste sensation.

DATE & DUKKAH BROWNIES

MAKES 16 PIECES

350 g (12 oz) pitted dates, coarsely chopped (or leave whole)
3 tablespoons hazelnut dukkah (see page 212)
300 g (10½ oz) bitter dark chocolate, coarsely chopped
80 g (2¾ oz) unsalted butter
4 eggs, whisked
300 g (10½ oz) caster (superfine) sugar
55 g (2 oz) plain (all-purpose) flour
3 tablespoons unsweetened cocoa powder, plus extra for dusting
2 teaspoons baking powder
100 g (3½ oz) sour cream
150 g (5½ oz/1 cup) dark chocolate melts

Preheat the oven to 170°C (325°F). Line a 20 cm x 30 cm (8 inch x 12 inch) baking tin with baking paper.

Put the dates, dukkah and 200 ml (7 fl oz) water in a medium saucepan over medium–high heat and bring to the boil. Set aside to cool. (This step can be done in advance.)

Put the chopped chocolate and butter in a heatproof bowl over a saucepan of simmering water, making sure that the water doesn't touch the base of the bowl. Stir until melted. Alternatively, melt the chocolate and butter in a microwave. Set aside to cool to room temperature.

Put the egg and sugar in a large bowl and mix until smooth. Add the cooled chocolate and butter mixture and stir until combined.

Sift together the flour, cocoa powder and baking powder into a medium bowl. Add to the chocolate mixture and stir with a wooden spoon. Add the sour cream, chocolate melts and the date and dukkah mixture, including the cooking liquid, and mix to combine.

Pour the mixture into the prepared tin. Bake for 40 minutes, or until set.

Allow the brownie to cool for at least 3 hours or until it is firm enough to cut. Dust with cocoa powder and cut into 16 squares.

Another take on baklava, this time utterly decadent. My recipe makes four individual logs but you can easily make one large tray – follow the method below but use eight sheets of filo on the base, add the chocolate and pistachio mixture, then put eight sheets of filo on top. You'll also need to pre-cut the baklava into diamond shapes prior to baking.

CHOCOLATE & PISTACHIO BAKLAVA

MAKES 24 PIECES

400 g (14 oz) pistachio nut kernels,
    coarsely chopped
200 g (7 oz) dark chocolate,
    coarsely chopped
4 tablespoons caster
    (superfine) sugar
2 teaspoons ground cinnamon
½ teaspoon freshly grated nutmeg
16 sheets filo pastry
170 g (6 oz) butter, melted

SYRUP
220 g (7¾ oz/1 cup) caster
    (superfine) sugar
1 tablespoon lemon juice
2 teaspoons rosewater

Preheat the oven to 170°C (325°F). Line a roasting tin with baking paper. (A roasting tin is preferable to a tray to catch the hot syrup.)

Pulse the pistachios in a food processor to a rough crumb (don't overprocess to a powder), then transfer to a large bowl. Pulse the chocolate in the food processor and add to the pistachios, along with the sugar, cinnamon and grated nutmeg. Mix well, and divide into 4 equal portions.

You will need 4 sheets of filo pastry per log. Lay a clean tea towel (dish towel) on a work surface. Lay a sheet of filo on the tea towel, the long side towards you. Brush with melted better. Repeat with 3 more sheets of filo to make a stack. Working on the long side closest to you, put a portion of the pistachio and chocolate mixture a quarter of the way along the filo stack, leaving a small gap at either end. Tightly roll the stack of filo sheets away from you to create a log. Put the log in the prepared tin, seam side down. Repeat to make 3 more logs. Brush with the remaining melted butter. Bake for 25–30 minutes, or until golden brown.

Meanwhile, make the syrup. Bring the sugar and 250 ml (9 fl oz/1 cup) water to the boil in a medium saucepan over medium–high heat. Reduce the heat to low and simmer for 15 minutes. Add the lemon juice and rosewater, increase the heat to medium–high and boil for 2–3 minutes. Set aside.

When the baklava is cooked, remove from the oven and immediately ladle over as much hot syrup as it can absorb. Leave in the tin for 3–4 minutes, then transfer to a wire rack. Cut into thick slices using a serrated knife.

I love these addictive brownies. They combine two of my favourite sweet ingredients – dark chocolate and sweet gooey halva – so I try to make them as often as possible.

CHOCOLATE HALVA BROWNIES

MAKES 16 PIECES

350 g (12 oz) plain halva, cut into
    2 cm (¾ inch) cubes
200 g (7 oz) dark chocolate,
    coarsely chopped
150 g (5½ oz) unsalted butter,
    coarsely chopped
4 eggs
300 g (10½ oz) caster
    (superfine) sugar
140 g (5 oz) plain (all-purpose) flour
20 g (¾ oz) unsweetened
    cocoa powder
½ teaspoon salt

Line a 20 cm x 30 cm (8 inch x 12 inch) baking tin with baking paper. Scatter the halva cubes evenly over the base of the tin.

Put the chocolate and butter in a heatproof bowl over a saucepan of simmering water, not letting the water touch the base of the bowl. Stir until melted. Alternatively, melt the chocolate and butter in a microwave. Set aside.

Put the eggs and sugar in a large bowl and whisk until the sugar has dissolved. Slowly pour the melted chocolate mixture over the egg mixture and stir until combined.

Sift the flour, cocoa powder and salt over the chocolate mixture and gently fold through. Pour the chocolate mixture over the halva cubes and gently spread over the base of the baking tin. Set aside to rest at room temperature for 30 minutes (this helps give the brownies a better crust). Preheat the oven to 180°C (350°F).

Bake the brownies for 20–25 minutes, or until they are set but still gooey in the centre. Cool on a wire rack. When completely cool, cut into 16 pieces.

STORAGE
Store in an airtight container for up to 1 week or freeze for up to 1 month.

So delicious, you can serve these little meringues with a bowl of cream and another of berry compote for dipping. Or rather than making individual meringues, make one large one and top with the cream and berry compote for a big chocolate berry pavlova.

CHOCOLATE MERINGUES

MAKES 12

120 g (4¼ oz) bitter dark chocolate
4 egg whites, at room temperature
220 g (7¾ oz/1 cup) caster (superfine) sugar
1 tablespoon white vinegar
1 tablespoon cornflour (cornstarch)

Preheat the oven to 140°C (275°F). Line a baking tray with greaseproof or baking paper.

Put the chocolate in a heatproof bowl over a saucepan of simmering water, making sure that the water doesn't touch the base of the bowl. Stir until melted. Alternatively, melt the chocolate in a microwave. Set aside to cool to room temperature.

Using an electric mixer with the whisk attachment, whisk the egg whites until soft peaks form. Slowly add the sugar and whisk until it forms a thick and glossy meringue.

Fold in the vinegar and cornflour, then swirl in the melted chocolate.

Spoon 2 heaped tablespoons of the mixture for each meringue onto the baking tray, leaving room for the meringues to expand during cooking.

Bake for 35–40 minutes, until the meringues are firm.

Remove from the oven and cool on a wire rack before serving.

The fig and walnut flavours go so well together in these lovely little cakes. You can make this recipe using a regular muffin or mini kugelhopf tray instead of the mini bundt tray we used here.

MINI FIG & WALNUT CAKES WITH MASCARPONE CHEESE

MAKES 8–10

150 g (5½ oz) walnuts
110 g (3¾ oz/¾ cup)
    self-raising flour
75 g (2½ oz/½ cup) plain
    (all-purpose) flour
250 g (9 oz) unsalted butter, cut into
    cubes, at room temperature
100 g (3½ oz) caster (superfine)
    sugar
80 g (2¾ oz) fig jam
3 eggs

TOPPING
250 g (9 oz) mascarpone cheese
250 ml (9 fl oz/1 cup) thin
    (pouring) cream
50 g (1¾ oz) icing
    (confectioners') sugar
5 fresh figs
50 g (1¾ oz) honey

Preheat the oven to 180°C (350°F). Thoroughly grease 10 holes of a mini bundt tray to prevent the cakes sticking when turned out.

Put the walnuts and self-raising and plain flours in a food processor and blend to a fine powder.

Using an electric mixer with the whisk attachment, cream the butter and sugar until pale and creamy. Add the jam and whisk for 2 minutes. Add the eggs one at a time, whisking well after each addition, and then whisk for an extra 2 minutes, or until really well combined. Fold in the walnut powder and mix until just combined.

Spoon the mixture into the tray, filling the holes to two-thirds of the way up. Bake for 20–25 minutes. Cool for 2–3 minutes in the tray then turn out onto a wire rack to cool.

To make the topping, put the mascarpone cheese, cream and icing sugar in a medium bowl and whisk until almost set, without overmixing.

Break the figs in half by hand. Spoon a dollop of cream onto each cake, and top with a fig half and a drizzle of honey.

A great carrot cake recipe is an essential in everyone's baking repertoire, and I can vouch for the popularity of this one. We make these cupcakes for the café but you can use the recipe to make two large 20 cm (8 inch) cakes and sandwich the topping in between.

CLASSIC KEPOS CARROT CUPCAKES

MAKES 8 LARGE OR 12 SMALL CUPCAKES

2 large carrots, grated
200 g (7 oz) dark brown sugar
150 ml (5 fl oz) light olive oil
2 eggs
100 g (3½ oz) walnuts,
    coarsely chopped
175 g (6 oz) self-raising flour, sifted
½ teaspoon bicarbonate of soda
    (baking soda)
½ teaspoon ground cinnamon
½ teaspoon ground ginger
½ teaspoon freshly grated nutmeg
½ teaspoon salt

TOPPING
150 g (5½ oz) cream cheese,
    at room temperature
300 g (10½ oz) icing (confectioners')
    sugar, sifted
zest of 1 lemon

Preheat the oven to 180°C (350°F). Line the holes of a muffin tray with 8 large or 12 small paper cases.

Put the carrot, sugar, olive oil and eggs in a large bowl and mix well to combine. Add the walnuts and fold through.

Put the flour, bicarbonate of soda, cinnamon, ginger, nutmeg and salt in a medium bowl and mix well. Gradually add the dry ingredients to the carrot mixture, stirring with a wooden spoon until just combined. Spoon the mixture into the paper cases and bake for 25–30 minutes.

Remove the cupcakes from the tray and cool on a wire rack. Meanwhile, using an electric mixer with the paddle attachment, beat the cream cheese until smooth. Gradually add the icing sugar and lemon zest and beat until combined. Spoon a dollop of the cream cheese icing onto each cupcake.

This recipe was given to me by my friend Michal, who helped when we were setting up Kepos Street Kitchen. She made these babka when we first opened, and the smell of them baking reminded me of the streets of Tel Aviv on a Friday afternoon, when most pastry shops would be cooking these cakes to get ready for the weekend.

MICHAL'S BABKA

MAKES 12 ROSETTES

500 g (1 lb 2 oz/3⅓ cups)
self-raising flour, plus
extra for dusting
25 g (1 oz) dried yeast
100 g (3½ oz) unsalted
butter, melted
115 g (4 oz) caster (superfine) sugar
3 tablespoons canola oil
2 eggs
90 ml (3 fl oz) lukewarm water

FILLING
190 g (6¾ oz) caster
(superfine) sugar
25 g (1 oz) unsweetened
cocoa powder
65 g (2¼ oz) unsalted butter,
at room temperature
3 tablespoons boiling water

To make the dough, put the flour, yeast, butter, sugar, oil, eggs and lukewarm water in a large bowl and mix to combine. Knead the mixture vigorously by hand on a lightly floured work surface for at least 10 minutes. Alternatively, use an electric mixer with the dough hook and mix for at least 6 minutes, or until the dough is smooth and sticky. (Stay close to the electric mixer to keep it steady as it will jump around while mixing this dough.)

Transfer the dough to a large clean bowl, dust the top with flour and cover the bowl with a damp tea towel (dish towel). Leave to prove in a warm place for at least 40 minutes, or until doubled in size.

Meanwhile, make the filling. Put the sugar, cocoa, butter and boiling water in a medium bowl and mix to combine.

Line a baking tray with baking paper. Dust a work surface with flour and roll out the proven dough to a large rectangle, approximately 5 mm (¼ inch) thick. Spread the filling over the dough, leaving a 1 cm (½ inch) border around the edge. Starting from the long edge closest to you, tightly roll the dough into a cylinder. Cut the cylinder into 12 equal portions. Place the babkas evenly on the prepared tray, 3 across and 4 down. Cover with a damp tea towel and leave to rise again for 40 minutes, or until doubled in size.

Preheat the oven to 180°C (350°F).

Bake for 30–40 minutes, or until golden. Serve warm.

DESSERT BANQUET

Sweets in the Middle East are a celebration in themselves. We generally won't have dessert after a big dinner, but instead sweets are a way of welcoming people into your home at other times of the day – we absolutely love the opportunity to make a lavish cake display for guests. Middle Eastern sweets and cakes tend to be sweeter than traditional Western desserts as they are being served on their own and become the meal. Nuts and dried and fresh fruits are also an integral part of the shared sweets table, with salted nuts working as the savoury part of the spread.

Adding orange blossom to a citrus-based dessert lifts and intensifies the beautiful aroma. And this slice tastes as good as it smells…

LEMON & ORANGE BLOSSOM SLICE

MAKES 12–16 PIECES

350 g (12 oz/2⅓ cups) plain
    (all-purpose) flour
pinch of salt
200 g (7 oz) cold unsalted
    butter, diced
125 g (4½ oz/1 cup) icing
    (confectioners') sugar,
    plus extra for dusting
1 egg
2 tablespoons cold water

TOPPING
zest and juice of 3 lemons
2 teaspoons orange blossom water
4 eggs
250 g (9 oz) caster (superfine) sugar
500 ml (17 fl oz/2 cups) thick
    (double) cream
100 g (3½ oz/⅔ cup) plain
    (all-purpose) flour, sifted
20 g (¾ oz) pistachio nut kernels,
    coarsely chopped

Preheat the oven to 170°C (325°F). Line a 20 cm x 30 cm (8 inch x 12 inch) baking tin with baking paper, allowing the excess to hang over the edge of the tin.

To make the base, put the flour, salt, butter, icing sugar, egg and water in a food processor and pulse until the mixture has a crumb-like appearance. Transfer to the prepared tin and spread over, pressing with your hands until the mixture is even. Bake for 25 minutes, or until golden brown. Allow to cool for 5–10 minutes.

Meanwhile, make the topping. Put the lemon zest and juice in a small bowl with the orange blossom water. Mix and set aside.

Put the eggs, sugar and cream in the bowl of an electric mixer and beat until well combined and fluffy. Gradually add the flour and combine gently. Add the lemon juice mixture and stir through.

Pour the topping over the base. Transfer to the oven and bake for 25 minutes, or until set.

Leave the slice to cool in the tin on a wire rack for at least 3 hours before cutting. Dust with icing sugar and sprinkle with pistachios.

Beautifully moist and with the real taste of almonds, this cake can be made in advance for a dinner party, or enjoyed for afternoon tea. It keeps refrigerated for up to a week, but I'm not sure it will last that long.

MARZIPAN CAKE

SERVES 8–10

6 eggs
300 g (10½ oz) unsalted
    butter, melted
270 g (9½ oz/2⅔ cups)
    almond meal
90 g (3¼ oz/1 cup)
    desiccated coconut
380 g (13½ oz) caster
    (superfine) sugar
½ teaspoon salt
1 vanilla bean, split lengthways and
    seeds scraped or 1 tablespoon
    vanilla bean paste
50 g (1¾ oz/½ cup) almond flakes

Preheat the oven to 170°C (325°F). Grease a 24 cm (9½ inch) spring-form cake tin and line the base with baking paper.

Put the eggs in a large bowl and whisk with a fork. Add the butter and mix until combined.

Put the almond meal, coconut, sugar, salt and vanilla bean seeds in a medium bowl and mix to combine. Add the almond meal mixture to the egg mixture and mix well. Pour into the cake tin and scatter the almond flakes over the top. Bake for 45 minutes, or until the cake is firm and golden brown.

Cool the cake in the tin on a wire rack for 10 minutes. Remove the spring-form ring and allow the cake to cool completely.

There was a food stand close to my childhood home that sold nothing but muhalbiyah. We kids loved the sugar rush we'd get from the cheap and tacky syrup with its artificial colouring, while the adults had a version made with grenadine syrup. Mine is a more sophisticated adult version, but still based on this childhood memory.

MUHALBIYAH WITH ROSEWATER (MILK PUDDING)

SERVES 4-6

1 litre (35 fl oz/4 cups) full-cream
    (whole) milk
80 g (2¾ oz) caster (superfine) sugar
70 g (2½ oz) cornflour (cornstarch)
2 tablespoons rosewater
100 g (3½ oz/¾ cup) pistachio
    nut kernels, toasted and
    coarsely chopped, to serve
fresh raspberries, to serve

SAUCE
300 g (10½ oz) fresh or
    frozen raspberries
50 g (1¾ oz) caster (superfine) sugar
1 tablespoon rosewater

Put the milk and sugar in a medium saucepan over medium–low heat and bring to the boil. Meanwhile, put the cornflour in a small bowl and add a few tablespoons of water, stirring until you have a gluggy wet mixture. Slowly add the cornflour to the hot milk, stirring with a wooden spoon, and reduce the temperature to low. Continue stirring for 8–10 minutes, or until the mixture has the consistency of a thick custard. Add the rosewater, stir and remove from the heat.

Pour the mixture into 4–6 serving glasses and allow to cool to room temperature. Transfer to the fridge and set overnight.

To make the sauce, put the raspberries and sugar in a food processor or blender and purée until smooth. Pass through a fine-mesh sieve to remove the seeds. Put the liquid in a small saucepan over low heat and bring to the boil. Simmer for 5 minutes then remove from the heat. Add the rosewater, stir and allow to cool.

When you are ready to serve, pour the sauce over the puddings and scatter with the pistachios and raspberries.

Use whatever dried fruit and nuts you like for this recipe, which is great eaten warm and fantastic eaten cold.

OUR FAVOURITE CROISSANT PUDDING

SERVES 6-8

4–5 large croissants
200 g (7 oz) chopped dried
    apricots or any dried fruit
    such as sultanas (golden
    raisins) or dates
3 eggs, whisked
395 g (14 oz) tin sweetened
    condensed milk
125 ml (4 fl oz/½ cup) thin
    (pouring) cream
375 ml (13 fl oz/1½ cups)
    full-cream (whole) milk
1 teaspoon vanilla bean paste
1 teaspoon ground cinnamon
small pinch of freshly
    grated nutmeg
100 g (3½ oz/¾ cup) pistachio nut
    kernels, lightly toasted and
    coarsely chopped

Preheat the oven to 180°C (350°F). Grease a 20 cm x 30 cm (8 inch x 12 inch) baking dish with butter.

Break the croissants into pieces and scatter over the base of the baking dish. Scatter over the apricot.

Put the egg, condensed milk, cream, milk, vanilla bean paste, cinnamon and nutmeg in a bowl and whisk to combine. Pour this mixture over the croissant pieces and apricot, pressing the dried apricots into the croissant.

Bake for 35 minutes, or until golden. Scatter the pistachios over the top. Serve warm or cold.

An unconventional pavlova that's perfect as a celebration cake, this was created accidentally one day at Kepos Street Kitchen when we were trying to make a unique gluten-free cake for a customer. It is a versatile recipe so you can change the type of nuts and berries you use – don't be afraid to put your own stamp on it. You can also make it look more like a regular pavlova by omitting the glaze and adding cream, fresh nuts and pomegranate seeds. It can be made up to 5 days in advance – just glaze it on the day you want to eat it.

PERSIAN PAVLOVA

SERVES 8-12

6 egg whites, at room temperature
200 g (7 oz) caster (superfine) sugar
500 g (1 lb 2 oz) plain halva, diced
    into 1 cm (½ inch) cubes
200 g (7 oz) pitted dates, chopped
200 g (7 oz) dried barberries
    or cranberries
125 g (4½ oz/1¼ cups) almond meal
50 g (1¾ oz) pistachio nut kernels,
    coarsely chopped
50 g (1¾ oz) blanched whole
    almonds, coarsely chopped
120 g (4¼ oz) white chocolate chips
1 teaspoon rosewater
shaved halva, chopped pistachio
    nut kernels, pomegranate seeds
    or rose petals dusted with sugar,
    to garnish (optional)

WHITE CHOCOLATE GLAZE
75 ml (2¼ fl oz) thin (pouring) cream
150 g (5½ oz) white chocolate,
    coarsely chopped

Preheat the oven to 160°C (315°F). Grease a 24 cm (9½ inch) spring-form cake tin with butter and line the base with baking paper.

Using an electric mixer with the whisk attachment, whisk the egg whites on high speed until soft peaks form. Gradually add the sugar, whisking until the mixture is firm and glossy as you would with a meringue.

Gently fold in the halva, dates, berries, almond meal, pistachios, almonds, chocolate chips and rosewater. Spoon the mixture into the prepared tin. Bake for 1 hour, or until it is firm to the touch. Set aside to cool completely in the tin on a wire rack.

To make the glaze, put the cream and chocolate in a small saucepan over low heat, stirring until melted. Remove from the heat and set aside to cool, stirring every 2 minutes to prevent lumps forming.

When ready to serve, remove the spring-form ring and spoon the glaze over the pavlova. Scatter over a Middle Eastern garnish, such as shaved halva, chopped pistachio nut kernels, pomegranate seeds or rose petals dusted with sugar, if desired.

An Arabic classic that has been adopted in Israel, which everyone has their own take on. Usually it is made with a semi-hard goat's cheese similar to mozzarella in its gooeyness, but I find this a little too rich so I use ricotta instead. Kataifi pastry, which can be found in Middle Eastern grocery stores and some supermarkets, is made of a beautiful type of dried noodle. Once combined with these ingredients and baked, it has a wonderful crunch, and soaks up the other flavours. In the Middle East this dish is traditionally eaten as a meal on its own.

RICOTTA CHEESE KANAFEH

SERVES 6-8

300 g (10½ oz) ricotta cheese, strained to remove excess liquid
100 g (3½ oz) buffalo mozzarella, grated
100 g (3½ oz) ghee
200 g (7 oz) kataifi noodles

SYRUP
150 g (5½ oz) caster (superfine) sugar
1 teaspoon rosewater

Preheat the oven to 160°C (315°F). Grease two 28 cm (11¼ inch) ovenproof frying pans.

Put the ricotta and mozzarella cheeses in a medium bowl and mix to combine. Set aside.

Melt the ghee in a small saucepan over medium–low heat.

Using your hands, shred the kataifi noodles into loose threads into a medium bowl. Pour the melted ghee over the noodles and mix well.

Put half of the noodles in one of the greased frying pans and spread over the base and up the side. Spread all of the cheese mixture over the noodles. Top with the remaining noodles and spread to cover the cheese. Cook in the oven for 30 minutes, or until golden brown.

Remove the pan from the oven and gently invert the noodle cake into the second greased frying pan. Cook in the oven for a further 10 minutes, or until golden.

To make the syrup, put the sugar and 200 ml (7 fl oz) water in a medium saucepan over medium heat. When the sugar has dissolved, bring to the boil and cook for 5 minutes, or until you get a syrupy consistency. Remove the saucepan from the heat, add the rosewater and stir to combine.

Pour the warm syrup over the warm noodle and cheese cake and serve immediately.

Tiramisu is one of those comforting desserts that simply works so well to end any meal. I've added a nice Middle Eastern twist with the halva, which gives it a nice crumble that's a textural surprise.

TIRAMISU

SERVES 8-10

5 eggs, separated
120 g (4¼ oz) caster
   (superfine) sugar
500 g (1 lb 2 oz) mascarpone cheese
2½ tablespoons Frangelico
   (optional)

BASE
400 g (14 oz) savoiardi (lady fingers/
   sponge finger biscuits)
100 g (3½ oz) dark (semisweet)
   chocolate chips
100 g (3½ oz) halva, broken into
   small pieces
100 g (3½ oz/¾ cup) pistachio
   nut kernels, chopped
400 ml (14 fl oz) black coffee,
   at room temperature
unsweetened cocoa powder,
   for dusting

Use an electric mixer with a whisk attachment to whisk the egg yolks until creamy.

Put the sugar and 2½ tablespoons water in a small saucepan and heat to 117°C (243°F), until it becomes a syrup. Gradually pour the sugar syrup into the egg yolk mixture while mixing on high speed. Continue whisking until the mixture is cool. Add the mascarpone cheese and Frangelico, if using, and mix until just combined. Transfer the mixture to a separate large bowl.

Put the egg whites in a clean dry bowl. Whisk until soft peaks form. Add to the cheese mixture and slowly fold in using a spatula.

To make the base, break the savoiardi into small crumbs. Put in a bowl with the chocolate chips, halva, pistachios and coffee.

To serve, use clean glass jars or small glasses. Put in a layer of the biscuit mixture followed by a layer of the cheese mixture. Continue layering until you reach the top of the jar. Set aside in the fridge for 1 hour. Dust with cocoa powder before serving.

As you may have gathered, I really love incorporating nuts into my recipes – and if I can add them to a cheesecake, I will. The pine nuts make this one extra special, along with the saffron. The flavour of the saffron is honey-like and develops as the cheesecake bakes.

SAFFRON & PINE NUT CHEESECAKE

SERVES 8–10

250 g (9 oz) digestive/wholemeal
    biscuits (graham crackers)
50 g (1¾ oz/⅓ cup) pine nuts,
    lightly toasted
100 g (3½ oz) unsalted
    butter, melted
750 g (1 lb 10 oz) cream cheese,
    at room temperature
250 g (9 oz) caster (superfine) sugar
2 tablespoons plain
    (all-purpose) flour
4 egg yolks
125 g (4½ oz) mascarpone cheese
1 vanilla bean, split lengthways
    and seeds scraped
1 tablespoon lemon juice
pinch of salt
pinch of saffron threads, soaked
    in 2 tablespoons hot water

Preheat the oven to 170°C (325°F). Grease a 24 cm (9½ inch) spring-form cake tin and line the base with baking paper.

Put the biscuits and pine nuts in the bowl of a food processor and pulse to a fine crumb. Transfer to a bowl and add the butter. Mix to combine, then press into the base and about three-quarters up the side of the prepared tin. Refrigerate for at least 2 hours or until firm.

Put the cream cheese, sugar and flour in the bowl of an electric mixer with the paddle attachment and mix until smooth and well combined. Add the egg yolks one at a time, beating well after each addition. Add the mascarpone cheese, vanilla seeds, lemon juice, salt and the saffron and its soaking water and mix until combined, scraping down the sides of the bowl.

Spoon the cream cheese mixture onto the biscuit base and bake for 45 minutes, or until the cheesecake is firm but still slightly wobbly. Allow to cool in the tin on a wire rack before serving.

I like using a bundt or kugelhopf cake tin for this recipe – it gives the cake a nice 'nana' look. But you can just as easily use a 24 cm (9½ inch) round cake tin. You can serve it with a dollop of natural yoghurt or enjoy it with a cup of mint and lemon tea (see page 199).

TAHINI & SESAME TEACAKE

SERVES 8-10

4 tablespoons tahini, for brushing, plus 200 g (7 oz) extra

5 tablespoons sesame seeds, for coating, plus 2 tablespoons extra

3 eggs

300 g (10½ oz) caster (superfine) sugar

1 vanilla bean, split lengthways and seeds scraped

190 ml (6½ fl oz) light extra virgin olive oil

240 ml (8 fl oz) orange juice

280 g (10 oz) plain (all-purpose) flour

2 teaspoons baking powder

Preheat the oven to 160°C (315°F). Brush the sides of a kugelhopf or fluted ring (bundt) cake tin with 4 tablespoons of tahini and evenly sprinkle with 5 tablespoons of sesame seeds. The oily tahini will help the cooked cake to slide out easily.

Put the eggs, sugar and vanilla seeds in a large bowl and mix using a wooden spoon. Slowly add the oil, stirring. Add the orange juice and stir to combine. Add 200 g tahini and mix well.

Sift the flour and baking powder over the wet ingredients and mix until just combined. Do not overmix. Add the extra 2 tablespoons of sesame seeds and fold in. Pour the mixture into the prepared tin and bake for 50 minutes, or until golden and firm.

Allow the cake to cool in the tin for 10 minutes. Turn out onto a wire rack to cool completely.

Based on an Eton Mess, this spectacular dessert combines the lovely crunch of kataifi pastry with luscious cream and seasonal berries. The separate elements can be prepared ahead of time and then assembled just before serving to make an impressive dish with minimum effort. Rather than trying to cut it, scoop out each portion with a large spoon and serve in bowls.

LAYERED KATAIFI, MASCARPONE & FRESH BERRIES

SERVES 8-10

250 g (9 oz) kataifi pastry
70 g (2½ oz) butter, melted
2 tablespoons caster (superfine) sugar
canola oil spray for cooking
500 g (1 lb 2 oz) mascarpone cheese
50 g (1¾ oz) icing (confectioners') sugar, plus 2 tablespoons extra
250 ml (9 fl oz/1 cup) thin (pouring) cream
800 g (1 lb 12 oz) mixed fresh berries
2–3 tablespoons pomegranate molasses (see page 229, optional)

Put the kataifi pastry in a large mixing bowl and pull apart the noodles with your hands. Add the melted butter and caster sugar and mix well by hand. Divide the mixture into 3 equal parts. Preheat the oven to 170°C (325°F).

Spray a 20 cm (8 inch) round cake tin well with canola oil. Take one portion of the kataifi mixture and spread it over the base of the tin, pushing it in and flattening the edge so the base is completely covered. Bake for 15–20 minutes, until the disc is lightly golden. Remove carefully from the tin and cool on a wire rack. Repeat with the remaining 2 portions so you have 3 baked discs.

To make the filling, put the mascarpone cheese, 50 g of icing sugar and the cream in a large bowl. Whisk together until thick and well combined, taking care not to overmix.

In a separate bowl, combine the mixed berries, the remaining icing sugar and the pomegranate molasses, if using, and carefully mix to combine, taking care not to crush the berries.

Assemble the dish on a serving platter or cake stand just before serving. Put 1 disc on the plate and top with a few spoonfuls of the mascarpone cream, pushing it almost to the edge of the disc, and scatter over a third of the berries. Add the second disc and repeat with more mascarpone cream and another third of the berries. Top with the last disc and the remaining mascarpone cream and berries.

CHAPTER SEVEN
DRINKS & TEAS

SHARING TEAS AND DRINKS IS CENTRAL TO OUR CULTURE.

It's all part of the ritual of getting together and enjoying each other's company. Including refreshing fruit concoctions, soothing teas and delicious cocktails, this chapter is a mixture of traditional and more contemporary drinks that have been developed over the years with Kepos Street Kitchen Bar Manager Ladislav Smid.

The flavours of watermelon and cucumber have a great affinity with each other, and this easy-to-make drink is incredibly refreshing on a hot summer's evening.

CUCUMBER & WATERMELON COOLER

MAKES 4

700 g (1 lb 9 oz/4 cups) cubed
    seedless watermelon
2 Lebanese (short) cucumbers or
    1 telegraph (long) cucumber,
    coarsely cut into cubes
3 tablespoons raw sugar syrup
    (see page 231)
juice of 2 limes
crushed ice
400 ml (14 fl oz) soda water
    (club soda)
watermelon pieces and cucumber
    slices, to garnish

Put the watermelon, cucumber, sugar syrup and lime juice in a large pitcher. Gently mash the mixture with a muddler. Top with crushed ice and soda water. Pour into four glasses and garnish with the watermelon and cucumber slices.

1. CUCUMBER & WATERMELON COOLER. 2. STRAWBERRY ROSEWATER FIZZ (RECIPE PAGE 190). 3. HOMEMADE LEMONADE (RECIPE PAGE 190).

The delicious combination of fresh strawberries with lemon zest and a hint of rosewater makes this one of our most popular drinks at Kepos Street Kitchen.

STRAWBERRY ROSEWATER FIZZ

MAKES 4

200 g (7 oz/1⅓ cup) hulled
    strawberries
100 ml (3½ fl oz) raw sugar syrup
    (see page 231)
zest of 1 lemon
1 tablespoon rosewater
crushed ice
400 ml (14 fl oz) soda water
    (club soda)
4 extra strawberries, to garnish

Put the strawberries, sugar syrup, lemon zest and rosewater in a blender and blend to a smooth purée. Fill four large glasses to just under halfway with the purée. Top with crushed ice and soda water and stir well. Make a strawberry flower to garnish. (Keep the green hull on the strawberries. Cut a cross about halfway into the bottom of each strawberry and carefully peel back each quarter to look like the petals of a flower.)

We turned this classic old recipe into an even more refreshing lemonade by adding a hint of orange blossom water.

HOMEMADE LEMONADE

MAKES 4

peel and juice of 8 lemons
2 teaspoons orange blossom water
280 ml (10 fl oz) raw sugar syrup
    (see page 231)
chilled soda water (club soda)
ice cubes
mint sprigs and lemon slices,
    to garnish

Put the lemon peel and juice, orange blossom water and sugar syrup in a blender and blend well. Transfer the lemonade syrup to a bottle and keep in the fridge for up to 1 week.

To serve, dilute 1 part syrup with 3–4 parts soda water to taste and top with ice cubes. Garnish with mint sprigs and lemon slices.

The Middle Eastern twist on this classic cocktail comes with the addition of silan (Israeli date 'honey') and dates.

DATE DAIQUIRI

MAKES 4

crushed ice
125 ml (4 fl oz/½ cup) Havana Club
    3-year-old white rum
3 tablespoons Maraschino liqueur
juice of 2 lemons
2 tablespoons silan (Israeli date
    'honey', see page 224)
caster (superfine) sugar, to garnish
4 dates, to garnish

Fill a cocktail shaker with crushed ice. Add the rum, liqueur, lemon juice and silan. Shake well.

Dip the rim of four chilled martini glasses in sugar.

Double-strain the drink into the martini glasses. Skewer the dates and use to garnish the cocktails.

This drink combines PAMA (a liqueur made from pomegranate juice, vodka and tequila) with sparkling wine and wild hibiscus flowers to create a refreshing cocktail. It's great on a hot day – or whatever the weather, really!

POMEGRANATE ROYALE

MAKES 4

4 wild hibiscus flowers in syrup
    (available from liquor stores
    and online)
4 tablespoons PAMA liqueur
600 ml (21 fl oz) sparkling wine

Place a wild hibiscus flower in the bottom of four champagne flutes and stand the flowers upright. Add 1 tablespoon of the PAMA liqueur to each glass and top with the sparkling wine. Pour a little hibiscus syrup into each glass; this will graduate from crimson at the bottom to a beautiful light pink at the top of the glass.

Quench your thirst with this beautiful combination of sweet and bitter flavours, with a hint of basil to add a refreshing edge.

GRAPEFRUIT & BASIL SODA

MAKES 4

2 pink grapefruit, cut into quarters
16 basil leaves
125 ml (4 fl oz/½ cup) raw sugar
    syrup (see page 231)
crushed ice
400 ml (14 fl oz) soda water
    (club soda)
basil sprigs and pink grapefruit
    slices, to garnish

Put 2 grapefruit quarters and 4 basil leaves in each of four glasses or mason drinking jars and muddle. Add the sugar syrup and fill the glasses with crushed ice. Top with the soda water and stir vigorously. Garnish with basil sprigs and grapefruit slices.

Our Bar Manager Ladislav created this mocktail based on a classic French cocktail made with pear vodka and elderflower liqueur.

PEAR & ELDERFLOWER SPRITZER

MAKES 4

160 ml (5¼ fl oz) elderflower cordial
    (available from delicatessens)
4 pears, juiced
crushed ice
400 ml (14 fl oz) soda water
    (club soda)
pear slices, to garnish

Put the elderflower cordial and pear juice in a small pitcher and stir to combine. Put crushed ice in four glasses, pour over the pear and elderflower mixture, top with soda water and stir well. Garnish with the pear slices.

1. GRAPEFRUIT & BASIL SODA. 2. POMEGRANATE MOJITO (RECIPE PAGE 194). 3. PEAR & ELDERFLOWER SPRITZER.

The mojito is a traditional Cuban cocktail but we've given it a Middle Eastern twist by adding the pomegranate. This recipe is non-alcoholic, but you can easily make it adults-only by adding 2 tablespoons of Havana Club 3-year-old white rum to each glass with the pomegranate juice. Use tall and fairly solid glasses that won't break when you are muddling in them.

POMEGRANATE MOJITO

MAKES 4

2 limes, cut into quarters
2 tablespoons fresh
    pomegranate pearls
3 tablespoons raw sugar syrup
    (see page 231)
4 mint sprigs
125 ml (4 fl oz/½ cup) fresh
    pomegranate juice
crushed ice
400 ml (14 fl oz) soda water
    (club soda)
extra mint leaves and
    pomegranate seeds, to garnish

Put 2 lime quarters, 2 teaspoons pomegranate seeds, ¾ tablespoon sugar syrup and a sprig of mint leaves into each of four glasses. Gently mash the mixture with a muddling stick. (The mint leaves should be bruised to release the essential oils but not shredded.) Add the pomegranate juice and stir to dissolve the sugar and lift the mint up from the bottom of the glasses. Top with crushed ice and soda water. Garnish with the extra mint leaves and pomegranate seeds.

FRESH POMEGRANATE JUICE

MAKES 60-125 ML (2-4 FL OZ) JUICE PER POMEGRANATE

pomegranates, as required

Put a pomegranate on a work surface and place your palm firmly over it. Roll the pomegranate back and forth. (You'll hear crunching inside the fruit as the membranes break.)

Cut the pomegranate in half. Hold one half over a bowl and squeeze so the juice and seeds stream out. Use a spoon to dislodge any stubborn seeds. Repeat with the other half. Discard any white membrane in the bowl and strain the mixture.

Arak is a potent spirit that originates from Iraq and is popular throughout the Mediterranean. Similar to the French pastis, Italian anisette, Spanish ojén, Turkish raki and Greek ouzo, arak is a clear and colourless aperitif that contains as much as 63 per cent alcohol. Recipes vary, and Iraqis may make it by fermenting date juice, the Levantine people use grapes, and the brew may also be produced from potatoes, figs or grains. There is even an Iranian version called Aragh-e Sagi ('dog's sweat') that skips the anise flavouring altogether.

POMELO ARAK

MAKES 4

juice and peel of 2 pink grapefruit
170 ml (5½ fl oz/⅔ cup) arak
3 tablespoons raw sugar syrup
    (see page 231)
2 teaspoons orange blossom water
crushed ice
mint leaves, to garnish

Make twists from the grapefruit peel.

Put the grapefruit juice, arak, sugar syrup and orange blossom water in a cocktail shaker and shake vigorously.

Fill four glasses with crushed ice and strain the grapefruit mixture over it. Garnish with mint leaves and a grapefruit peel twist.

This lightly floral-tasting tea is perfect to serve at afternoon tea with Middle Eastern cakes and sweets.

ROSE PETAL TEA

MAKES 4

2 cups rose petals (fresh and
    pesticide-free)
1 litre (35 fl oz/4 cups) distilled water
honey, to taste

Rinse the rose petals under cold running water and gently pat dry with paper towel. Put the petals in a large saucepan with the distilled water over medium–high heat. Bring to the boil then reduce the heat to low and simmer for 5 minutes, or until the rose petals darken in colour.

Strain into a teapot or cups and add honey to taste.

Famous for the way it is made, Turkish coffee is prepared in an ibrik (cezve) – a special small coffee pot that is heated. You can use any small saucepan to make it, however. Sugar is optional but added during the brewing process, not after, if you're having it. Cream or milk is never added to Turkish coffee, which is always served in demitasse (100–150 ml/3½–5 fl oz) cups. In some regions, your fortune is told using the coffee grinds left in the cup.

TURKISH COFFEE

MAKES 4

sugar to taste (optional)
4 tablespoons extra finely
    ground Arabic coffee
    (powder consistency)
½ teaspoon ground cardamom
    or 4 cardamom pods

Put 1 litre (35 fl oz/4 cups) water and sugar to taste in an ibrik or small saucepan. Bring to the boil over medium–high heat. When boiling, remove from the heat and add the coffee and cardamom.

Return the ibrik or saucepan to the heat and bring back to the boil. Remove it from the heat again when the coffee foams. After 1 minute, return it to the heat again, allowing it to foam, then remove it from the heat again.

Pour the coffee into four cups and allow it to sit for 1–2 minutes so the grounds can settle to the bottom of the cup. If you used a cardamom pod you can leave it in the cup for added flavour or remove it.

NOTES
Tips for making Turkish coffee:
* Always serve Turkish coffee with foam on top, as this keeps the coffee tasting fresh.
* If you can't find finely ground Arabic coffee, you can buy a bag of coffee beans at a coffee seller and ask them to grind it to a powder-like consistency for Turkish coffee.
* Do not stir the coffee after pouring it into the cups as the foam will collapse.
* Always start with cold water.
* I make my coffee the traditional way, as above, but you can omit one of the foaming steps if you like.

1. TURKISH COFFEE. 2. SPICY TEA/FINJAN ERFEH (RECIPE PAGE 199).
3. SPICED HOT CHOCOLATE (RECIPE PAGE 198).

Ground spices and cinnamon sticks add flavour to this delicious drink that can be served all year round, not just in winter.

SPICED HOT CHOCOLATE

MAKES 4

4 tablespoons unsweetened
   cocoa powder
75 g (2¼ oz/⅓ cup) caster
   (superfine) sugar
½ teaspoon ground cinnamon
pinch of freshly grated nutmeg
pinch of salt
125 ml (4 fl oz/½ cup) hot water
875 ml (30 fl oz/3½ cups) full-cream
   (whole) milk
1 teaspoon natural vanilla extract
4 cinnamon sticks, to garnish

Put the cocoa powder, sugar, cinnamon, nutmeg and salt in a medium saucepan over medium heat. Add the hot water, stir and bring the mixture to the boil. Boil, stirring constantly, for 2 minutes. Gradually add the milk and continue stirring until it has warmed through, without bringing to the boil.

Remove the saucepan from the heat, add the vanilla and stir. Serve the hot chocolate in four mugs with the cinnamon sticks.

There are many types of tea on offer in the Middle East, often served for different occasions. This spicy tea is traditionally served to guests who come to visit a newborn baby.

SPICY TEA (FINJAN ERFEH)

MAKES 4

1½ tablespoons anise seeds
3 cinnamon sticks
2 whole cloves
½ teaspoon ground ginger
sugar, to taste
toasted whole walnuts, to garnish

Put 1 litre (35 fl oz/4 cups) water in a large saucepan over medium–high heat. Add the anise seeds, cinnamon sticks, cloves and ginger and bring to the boil. Reduce the heat to low and steep for 10–15 minutes.

Strain into four cups, add sugar to taste and garnish with walnuts.

The tartness of lemon and distinctive flavour of mint transform black tea, making it a perfect complement to many Middle Eastern dishes.

MINT & LEMON TEA

MAKES 4

4 teabags (any type of black tea)
2 teaspoons grated lemon peel
4 mint sprigs

Put 1 litre (35 fl oz/4 cups) water in a medium saucepan over medium–high heat and bring to the boil. Add the teabags, lemon peel and mint. Cover with a lid, turn off the heat and allow to steep for 10 minutes.

Strain into a teapot or four cups and serve immediately.

LADISLAV SMID, BAR MANAGER

This refreshing drink is popular in summer. It's also versatile – you can change the flavour by adding rosewater or orange blossom water instead of mastic, for example. The Turks add noodles to almond milk and call it 'falooda'.

ALMOND MILK

MAKES 1 LITRE (35 FL OZ/4 CUPS)

480 g (1 lb 1 oz/3 cups) blanched almonds
1 litre (35 fl oz/4 cups) boiling water
160 g (5¾ oz) caster (superfine) sugar
¼ teaspoon mastic powder

Put almonds in a large bowl and add the boiling water. Set aside for 30–45 minutes, or until the water cools to room temperature. Drain and discard the water.

Put the soaked almonds, 1 litre (3 fl oz/4 cups) room-temperature water, sugar and mastic in a blender and blend to as fine a mixture as possible. Transfer to the fridge to infuse for 3 hours.

Pass the almond milk through a piece of muslin (cheesecloth) or a chinois strainer. Discard the ground almonds and keep the milk. It will keep refrigerated for up to 1 week.

Traditionally served warm, saffron milk is also nice chilled and served over ice.

SAFFRON MILK

MAKES 4

2 litres (70 fl oz/8 cups) full-cream (whole) milk
55 g (2 oz/¼ cup) caster (superfine) sugar
1½ tablespoons saffron threads

Put the milk, sugar and saffron threads in a large saucepan over medium–high heat. Bring to the boil, stirring constantly to prevent sticking. Allow the milk to boil for 3–5 minutes, or until the saffron has dissolved. Remove from the heat, pour into four mugs and allow to cool to warm drinking temperature.

CHAPTER EIGHT

KITCHEN FUNDAMENTALS

THESE RECIPES ARE THE ONES I COME BACK TO TIME AND TIME AGAIN – THEY ARE THE CORNERSTONES OF MY CUISINE.

I'm sure you will also want to make them for snacks and to use in other ways, beyond the ideas here. But first a friendly word of encouragement: don't be put off by the length of some of these recipes. I promise you won't be stuck in the kitchen for hours – it may be that you'll be measuring or chopping for just a little longer than for the express, in-a-flash meals offered in many modern cookbooks, but the rewards are worth it.

A beautifully coloured dip with an earthy flavour that is balanced with the delicacy of the goat's curd.

BEETROOT, CUMIN & GOAT'S CURD DIP

MAKES 550 G (1 LB 4 OZ)

1 large beetroot (beet), trimmed
2 garlic cloves, peeled
1 teaspoon ground cumin
2½ tablespoons olive oil
200 g (7 oz/¾ cup) goat's curd

Put the whole beetroot in a medium saucepan and cover with cold water. Bring to the boil over medium–high heat and boil until tender, around 30–45 minutes, depending on the size of the beetroot.

Drain the beetroot and allow it to cool until you are able to handle it. Peel off the skin and cut the flesh into chunks.

Put the beetroot, garlic and cumin in a food processor and blitz until you have a smooth paste. Slowly drizzle in the olive oil until it is combined.

Transfer to a medium bowl, season with salt and freshly ground black pepper and fold in the goat's curd.

Store this dip in an airtight container in the fridge for up to 5 days.

My green tahini is a take on the classic tahini – which is whiter in colour – and is used as a dressing, dip or a complement to hummus. The addition of more herbs in my version gives it a vibrant green colour, as well as a grassier flavour and fragrance that works well with many dishes.

GREEN TAHINI

MAKES 200 G (7 OZ)

2 cups coriander (cilantro), leaves
    coarsely chopped
125 ml (4 fl oz/½ cup) lemon juice
2 garlic cloves, peeled
90 g (3¼ oz/⅓ cup) tahini
1 teaspoon sea salt flakes

In a food processor, blend the coriander with 100 ml (3½ fl oz) water until you have a smooth green paste; don't overblend as the coriander will go black. Add the lemon juice, garlic and tahini and blend until smooth. Stir through the sea salt flakes.

Store this dip in an airtight container in the fridge for up to 5 days.

Definitely one for garlic lovers, toum is a traditional Middle Eastern dip that can also be served as a condiment with steak or chicken, or added as an extra seasoning to salad dressings. The quantity of garlic can be adjusted to taste.

TOUM

MAKES 200 G (7 OZ)

12 garlic cloves, peeled
1 teaspoon sea salt flakes
250 ml (9 fl oz/1 cup) olive oil
juice of 2 lemons

Put the garlic and salt in a food processor and blitz to a smooth paste. Slowly drizzle in the olive oil while the motor is running. The mixture will thicken and is ready when it resembles the same consistency of room-temperature butter.

Transfer to a mixing bowl and add the lemon juice to taste.

Toum will keep in an airtight container in the fridge for up to 2 weeks.

DIPS

Great when entertaining guests, a spread of dips can be made ahead of time and served with a variety of breads and seasonings, such as za'atar (see page 214). Any leftovers can be incorporated in a shared table of food, as all will complement most Middle Eastern dishes.

1 **TOUM** see page 205
2 **BEETROOT, CUMIN & GOAT'S CURD DIP** see page 204
3 **HUMMUS** see page 210
4 **GREEN TAHINI** see page 205
5 **LABNEH** see page 209

A wonderful soft cheese, labneh is one of the easiest and most satisfying things you can make at home. You can use natural or Greek-style yoghurt for this recipe – the natural yoghurt will give a much silkier texture and less acidic flavour than the Greek-style yoghurt. I suggest you try this recipe with both and pick the one you like the most. I love eating labneh with lots of good-quality olive oil, a sprinkle of za'atar (see page 214) or hazelnut dukkah (see page 212), and some hot bread.

LABNEH

MAKES 400 G (14 OZ)

1 teaspoon salt
1 kg (2 lb 4 oz) natural or
    Greek-style yoghurt
juice of ½ lemon (if you are using
    natural yoghurt)

Mix the salt through the yoghurt. Hang a piece of muslin (cheesecloth) over a large bowl and pour the yoghurt into the cloth.

Hang the yoghurt in the fridge suspended over the bowl and allow the yoghurt to drain for 2–3 days; the longer you allow it to hang, the firmer the labneh will be.

Minimally drained, unrolled and unmarinated labneh will keep for 5–7 days. Marinated labneh will last for up to 2 weeks.

NOTE
Once the labneh is firm, you can add different flavourings. Roll the labneh into tablespoon-size or larger balls and crust them in chilli flakes, mild paprika, dried garlic, oregano, dried mint, or whatever you like. Put the balls in a sterilised jar and top with olive oil, then store in the fridge. A beautifully wrapped jar of flavoured labneh balls is a great homemade gift.

Many countries claim hummus as their own but I believe it originated in the Ottoman Empire and then spread to the Middle East. There are many different ways of making it and everyone thinks their version is the best. Classic hummus recipes use a mortar and pestle to break down the chickpeas, which will give you a more grainy texture than the smooth version I like to make. I also like to add fresh lemon juice, as it gives a slightly acidic edge and makes a lighter colour. You can use tinned chickpeas but the result will not be as silky and smooth. If using tinned chickpeas, you will need 500 g (1 lb 2 oz) drained chickpeas – bring them to the boil, add the baking powder and cook for a further 5 minutes.

HUMMUS

MAKES ABOUT 1 KG (2 LB 4 OZ)

150 g (5½ oz) dried chickpeas
¼ teaspoon baking powder
5 garlic cloves, peeled
400 g (14 oz) raw tahini
1 teaspoon salt
pinch of ground cumin
100 ml (3½ fl oz) lemon juice

In a large saucepan or bowl, soak the chickpeas in cold water (at least 4 times the quantity of the dried chickpeas) for at least 12 hours – overnight is good. Change the water at least twice during this process.

Drain the chickpeas and rinse well. Transfer to a large saucepan with a lid. Cover with at least double the quantity of water to the chickpeas and bring to the boil. Cook over medium heat with the lid on for 2 hours, topping up the water as necessary.

After 2 hours, if the chickpeas are soft enough, add the baking powder. (If not, continue cooking until they soften up.) Cook for a further hour, or until the chickpeas start to break down but are not mushy.

Put the garlic in a food processor (don't use a stick blender) with 200 ml (7 fl oz) water and blend to a very smooth consistency. Put through a sieve and keep the liquid, discarding the puréed garlic.

Drain the chickpeas. Put them in the food processor and blend to a smooth paste; this will take 7–10 minutes. Add the tahini, reserved garlic water, salt and cumin and blend well, scraping down the side occasionally, and adding more water if necessary. Transfer to a large mixing bowl. Add the lemon juice and gently whisk in (you do not want to over-aerate the hummus and lose the dense consistency). Store in a sealed container in the fridge for up to 5 days.

Traditional dukkah, which is the Vegemite of Egypt, is made with peanuts rather than hazelnuts, and is eaten with olive oil and bread for breakfast. I love using roasted hazelnuts for my dukkah because they are nuttier in flavour and the skins are a beautiful colour. You can use peanuts or any other type of nut instead of hazelnuts.

HAZELNUT DUKKAH

MAKES 520 G (1 LB 2 OZ)

1¾ cups hazelnuts
1 tablespoon coriander seeds
1 tablespoon cumin seeds
1¼ cups sesame seeds
2 teaspoons sea salt flakes
2 teaspoons freshly ground
    black pepper

Preheat the oven to 160°C (315°F).

Put the hazelnuts on one baking tray, and the coriander and cumin seeds on a separate tray, and bake until toasted, approximately 15 minutes.

After the hazelnuts and seeds have been in the oven for 10 minutes, add the sesame seeds on a separate tray and toast for the remaining 5 minutes, or until lightly coloured. Remove all the trays from the oven and allow the nuts and seeds to cool to room temperature.

Put the hazelnuts in a food processor and pulse to a coarse breadcrumb size. (You could also crush the hazelnuts the traditional way using a mortar and pestle – good exercise for the biceps!) Transfer the hazelnuts to a large mixing bowl.

Put the cumin and coriander seeds in the food processor and process until almost a powder. (Use a mortar and pestle to do this if you prefer.)

Add this powder to the bowl along with the toasted sesame seeds, salt and pepper. Mix well using a wooden spoon.

Dukkah can be kept for up to a year – but I am sure you will eat it all before then! It is best stored in an airtight container in a cool, dry place.

A spice mix that can contain up to 30 different spices, ras el hanout originated from North Africa and loosely translated means 'top of the shop' in Arabic. My blend has fewer spices but is still beautifully aromatic.

RAS EL HANOUT

MAKES 100 G (3½ OZ)

1 tablespoon black peppercorns
2 teaspoons allspice berries or
    ground allspice
1 tablespoon coriander seeds
2 star anise
1 tablespoon ground mace
1 tablespoon ground cinnamon
1 tablespoon freshly grated nutmeg
1 tablespoon ground cloves
1 tablespoon ground ginger
2 teaspoons ground turmeric
2 teaspoons cayenne pepper

In a dry frying pan, lightly toast the black peppercorns, allspice berries (if using) and coriander seeds over low heat. Using a mortar and pestle, grind to a powder.

Combine all of the ingredients in a bowl and store in an airtight container for up to 2 months.

Although this Middle Eastern spice mixture has the name of the Arabic word for thyme, the actual za'atar leaf (which belongs to the same family of herbs) is closer to marjoram or oregano. However, because za'atar leaf is only available seasonally and not always easy to find – a specialised Middle Eastern grocery store may stock it – this recipe provides an excellent alternative.

ZA'ATAR

MAKES 40 G (1½ OZ)

2 handfuls thyme sprigs, dried and
    leaves picked or 1 large handful
    dried thyme (available in Middle
    Eastern or Greek grocery stores)
2 tablespoons ground sumac
2 teaspoons sea salt flakes
2 tablespoons sesame seeds,
    toasted

To dry the thyme leaves, preheat the oven to 50°C (120°F) or the lowest setting. Spread the thyme sprigs over a baking tray and let them dry out in the oven for 1 hour or more if necessary. When cool enough to handle, gently break off the leaves. Alternatively, you can spread the thyme sprigs out on a tea towel (dish towel) and dry them outside in the sun.

Combine all the ingredients and transfer to an airtight container. Store in a cool, dark place for up to a month.

Baharat is the Arabic word for spice, but what we call baharat is actually a spice blend. It can be used as a dry rub on meat, mixed with olive oil as a marinade or sprinkled to add depth of flavour when roasting vegetables.

BAHARAT

MAKES 100 G (3½ OZ)

2 tablespoons black peppercorns
2 tablespoons coriander seeds
2 tablespoons cumin seeds
1 tablespoon allspice berries
1 teaspoon cardamom pods
2 teaspoons ground cinnamon
2 teaspoons sweet paprika
½ teaspoon freshly grated nutmeg

In a small frying pan over medium–low heat, dry-fry the peppercorns, coriander and cumin seeds, allspice berries and cardamom pods until fragrant, around 4–5 minutes. Remove from the heat and put in a bowl. Add the remaining ingredients to the bowl and mix to combine.

Store in an airtight container for up to 2 weeks. It can be kept longer, but it will not be as fragrant or as fresh.

A great staple, these preserved lemons get better with time. They will last for over a year in your fridge, and you can make this recipe when lemons are in season and the best quality and price. When choosing lemons to preserve, pick the smallest, freshest ones with the thickest skin. You can add whatever you want – chilli for an extra kick, sweet paprika for extra colour – but I like the basic version because I can use the preserved lemons in any way I choose.

PRESERVED LEMONS

MAKES ABOUT 1 KG (2 LB 4 OZ)

1 kg (2 lb 4 oz) small lemons
1½ tablespoons sugar
⅔ cup rock salt
2½ tablespoons olive oil

Using a small sharp knife cut a cross in the lemons to about halfway down without cutting all the way through, to make a cavity to fill with the sugar and salt.

Combine the sugar and salt. Stuff the lemon cavities with the mixture.

Put the lemons into a 2 litre (70 fl oz/8 cup) preserving jar in layers, pressing them down as you go. Seal the jar and set aside at room temperature for 3–5 days to allow the lemons to release their juices.

Open the jar and add the olive oil, which will help to preserve the lemons from oxidisation. Leave the lemons for 1 week in a cool, dark place, then move the jar to the fridge and use the preserved lemons whenever needed.

Keep sealed in the fridge for up to 1 year or more.

Pickles are an essential condiment that are always included on the table in any Middle Eastern home. It is not considered a meal if there aren't any pickles!

BEETROOT PICKLED CUCUMBERS

MAKES ABOUT 1 KG (2 LB 4 OZ)

1 kg (2 lb 4 oz) baby (or smallest you can find) Lebanese (short) cucumbers
310 ml (10¾ fl oz/1¼ cups) red wine vinegar
8 tablespoons salt
1 tablespoon caster (superfine) sugar
1 large beetroot (beet), washed and trimmed
4 garlic cloves, peeled
1 handful dill, including stems, washed and drained

Wash the cucumbers well and set on a clean tea towel (dish towel) to dry.

Mix 1.5 litres (52 fl oz/6 cups) water with the vinegar, salt and sugar until the salt and sugar dissolve. This should taste salty like sea water.

Cut the beetroot into chunks (the smaller the chunks, the more colour you will have in the cucumbers) and layer in a sterilised 2 litre (70 fl oz/8 cup) jar with the whole cucumbers, garlic and dill. Pour the liquid over, seal and set aside for a week.

These pickled cucumbers can be stored in the sealed sterilised jar for up to 2 months. If keeping them for longer, it is best to pour a little olive oil on the top of the water.

CONDIMENTS

These jams and sauces are fundamental to Middle Eastern cooking. Make these, and you are creating the essence of the cuisine.

A versatile paste that can be used to marinate meat, fish and vegetables, chermoula will give your dishes a real flavour kick. I like to use it to marinate chicken, which I'll then grill on the barbecue.

CHERMOULA

MAKES 350 G (12 OZ)

2 tablespoons cumin seeds
2 tablespoons coriander seeds
1 tablespoon caraway seeds
1 brown onion, coarsely chopped
4 garlic cloves, peeled
2 handfuls coriander (cilantro), leaves, stems and roots washed well
1 large green chilli
1 preserved lemon (see page 216), skin only
3 teaspoons ground turmeric
2½ tablespoons lemon juice
100 ml (3½ fl oz) olive oil

Heat a frying pan over medium heat and dry-fry the cumin, coriander and caraway seeds until fragrant, around 3 minutes. Using a food processor, break the seeds down until coarse.

Add the onion, garlic, coriander, chilli, preserved lemon and turmeric to the food processor and blend to a smooth paste. Add the lemon juice and blend for a further 2 minutes.

Scrape down the side of the bowl. Keep the motor running as you slowly drizzle in the olive oil. Season to taste.

Put the chermoula in a sterilised jar and seal. Store in the fridge for up to 2 weeks.

A versatile condiment, this savoury jam is great on sandwiches,
with grilled meats or to build up flavour in Middle Eastern cooking.

CHILLI JAM

MAKES ABOUT 2 KG (4 LB 8 OZ)

3 tablespoons olive oil
200 g (7 oz) red bullet chillies,
    finely chopped
100 g (3½ oz) large red chillies,
    finely chopped
4 garlic cloves, finely chopped
850 g (1 lb 14 oz) red capsicums
    (peppers), seeded and chopped
    into 2 cm (¾ inch) dice
700 g (1 lb 9 oz) tomatoes, chopped
    into 2 cm dice
1 litre (35 fl oz/4 cups) white
    wine vinegar
15 g (½ oz) salt
1.5 kg (3 lb 5 oz) caster (superfine)
    sugar, or jam sugar with
    Jamsetta included
50 g (1¾ oz) Jamsetta, if using
    caster/superfine sugar

Heat the olive oil in a large saucepan over medium heat. Add the chillies and garlic and cook for 1–2 minutes, but do not allow to colour. Add the capsicum, tomato, vinegar and salt. Reduce the heat to low and simmer for 1 hour, stirring regularly.

Add the caster sugar or jam sugar and continue cooking for another hour, stirring from time to time.

Increase the heat and boil the mixture for 45 minutes, stirring regularly to prevent it from catching and burning.

Remove the saucepan from the heat and add the Jamsetta, if using, stirring until dissolved. Return the saucepan to the heat and cook for a further 30 minutes.

Bottle in sterilised jars and store in a cool, dark place for 2–3 months. Refrigerate once opened.

There are many versions of harissa recipes. This one makes a more vinegary style of harissa than the more traditional paste, but you can vary it by adding less oil and vinegar, and more chilli. I like to use this harissa as a dressing rather than cooking with it.

RED HARISSA

MAKES ABOUT 1 KG (2 LB 4 OZ)

700 g (1 lb 9 oz) capsicums
    (peppers), roasted, peeled
    and seeded
6 garlic cloves, peeled
2 large green chillies
2 handfuls coriander (cilantro),
    leaves and stems washed and
    coarsely chopped
3 teaspoons mild paprika
2 teaspoons ground cumin
2 teaspoons ground coriander
2 teaspoons caster (superfine) sugar
2½ tablespoons red wine vinegar
200 ml (7 fl oz) extra virgin olive oil

Put the roasted capsicums, garlic, chillies and chopped coriander in a food processor and blend to a paste. Add the paprika, cumin, ground coriander and sugar and blend for a further minute. Add the vinegar and salt to taste, then drizzle in the olive oil slowly with the motor running until combined.

Store in an airtight container in the fridge for up to 2 weeks.

Another savoury jam, this one works really well as a condiment with chicken liver pâté or to add a Middle Eastern twist to whatever you are cooking.

TOMATO & BAHARAT JAM

MAKES 800 G (1 LB 12 OZ)

600 g (1 lb 5 oz) tomatoes, blanched, peeled, seeded and chopped
200 g (7 oz) caster (superfine) sugar
3 star anise
2 whole cloves
4 cinnamon sticks
2 teaspoons tomato paste (concentrated purée)
juice of ½ lemon
1 teaspoon sea salt flakes

Put the tomato, sugar, star anise, cloves and cinnamon sticks in a large saucepan over medium heat and cook for 25 minutes, stirring from time to time. Reduce the heat to low, add the tomato paste and cook, stirring occasionally, for 20 minutes or until thickened. Add the lemon juice, salt and freshly ground black pepper to taste. Cook for a further 5 minutes.

Ladle the jam into sterilised jars and allow to cool. Store in the fridge for up to 2 weeks. Remove the star anise, cloves and cinnamon sticks before serving.

Spread this beautiful homemade honey substitute on toast for breakfast, bake it in cakes and use it in dressings for a different flavour. As the dates need to be soaked in water overnight, this recipe is made over two days.

SILAN (ISRAELI DATE 'HONEY')

MAKES ABOUT 2.25 KG (5 LB)

5 kg (11 lb) dates, pitted

Put the pitted dates in a large shallow dish. Add enough boiling water to cover the dates and set aside overnight.

When the dates are soft, transfer with the soaking liquid in batches to a blender and process to a smooth fine paste.

Put the date paste in a piece of muslin (cheesecloth) and, over a medium saucepan, squeeze out as much liquid as you can. You will need a fair amount of physical force to do this. Discard the date paste.

Place the saucepan with the date liquid over medium heat and bring to a simmer. Cook for 30 minutes, stirring every 5 minutes, and keeping the liquid at a slow simmer. After 30 minutes, reduce the heat to low and simmer until the liquid is very dark, intense and thick. Be careful not to over-reduce and burn.

Pour the 'honey' into sterilised jars. Store in a cool, dark place for up to 3 months. Store in the fridge once opened.

You can add this chilli paste to salads, have it with hummus, finish a stew with it or, as I love to do, add it to a risotto for a nice kick. It has so many uses, and green zhoug will last for a few weeks in the fridge.

GREEN ZHOUG

MAKES 600 G (1 LB 5 OZ)

15 large green chillies, chopped
10 garlic cloves, peeled
1 large handful coriander (cilantro), leaves and stems chopped
1 large handful flat-leaf (Italian) parsley, chopped
250 ml (9 fl oz/1 cup) olive oil

Put the chillies, garlic, coriander and parsley in a food processor and blend to a paste. Add the olive oil and salt to taste, and whiz to combine. Transfer to a sterilised jar and store in the fridge for up to 2 weeks.

The garlicky flavour of aïoli works perfectly where you'd use mayonnaise. The tart sumac version at the bottom of the page is a great substitute for tartare sauce, and is delicious with fish and chips. The egg whites left over can be used to make pavlova or meringues.

AÏOLI

MAKES 750 G (1 LB 10 OZ)

5 garlic cloves, peeled
5 egg yolks
1 teaspoon dijon mustard
½ teaspoon sea salt flakes
1 teaspoon white wine vinegar
500 ml (17 fl oz/2 cups) light olive oil

Preheat the oven to 170°C (325°F). Put the garlic on a baking tray and cook until lightly golden, about 7–8 minutes (if overcooked it will have a bitter taste). Cool the garlic to room temperature. Mash with a fork.

Blend the egg yolks, mustard, salt, vinegar and garlic in a blender or food processor until well combined and smooth, scraping down the side of the bowl. Very slowly, drizzle in the olive oil while the motor is running, until the aïoli is well emulsified and thick.

Always keep aïoli refrigerated. It will last in the fridge up to 7 days.

SUMAC AÏOLI

MAKES 450 G (1 LB)

2 egg yolks
1 teaspoon dijon mustard
2 tablespoons lemon juice
2 tablespoons husroum
    (white verjuice) or white
    balsamic vinegar
150 ml (5 fl oz) olive oil
150 ml (5 fl oz) vegetable oil
1 teaspoon salt
½ teaspoon sugar
2 teaspoons sumac

Blend the egg yolks, mustard, lemon juice and husroum in a blender or food processor until combined. Very slowly drizzle in the oils while the motor is running, until the mixture has thickened.

Transfer to a bowl, add the salt, sugar and sumac and mix gently. Cover with plastic wrap and keep refrigerated for up to 7 days.

There are two ways to prepare crisp pita bread, which is perfect for eating with hummus and other Middle Eastern dips. One is to bake it in the oven, but I prefer this more indulgent deep-fried version.

CRISP PITA BREAD

SERVES 4 AS AN ACCOMPANIMENT

2 pita breads (see page 47) or other flat Lebanese bread, or 2 sheets mountain bread
1 litre (35 fl oz/4 cups) rice bran oil
1 teaspoon sea salt flakes

Tear the bread into rough pieces approximately 5 cm x 10 cm (2 inches x 4 inches).

Put the rice bran oil in a deep frying pan and heat to 170°C (325°F), or when a cube of bread dropped into the oil turns golden brown in 20 seconds. Drop in 2 pieces of bread at a time and cook for 2–3 minutes, turning occasionally, until golden brown. Drain on paper towel and continue until all the bread is cooked.

Sprinkle the crisp pita bread with sea salt flakes and serve, or store in an airtight container lined with paper towel for up to 3 days.

Serve this ice cream with a rich dessert – like a flourless chocolate cake – or simply with Middle Eastern garnishes such as chopped pistachios or Turkish delight, pomegranate seeds, rose petals or even a drizzle of grenadine.

MASTIC ICE CREAM

MAKES ABOUT 2 LITRES (70 FL OZ/8 CUPS)

1.4 litres (49 fl oz) full-cream
    (whole) milk, plus 100 ml
    (3½ fl oz) extra
400 g (14 oz) caster
    (superfine) sugar
70 g (2½ oz) cornflour (cornstarch)
1 tablespoon mastic, pounded
    to a powder using a mortar
    and pestle
2 tablespoons rosewater

Pour the 1.4 litres of milk into a large saucepan and add the sugar. Place over medium heat and bring to a simmer, stirring.

Meanwhile, combine the cornflour with the extra milk until smooth.

Reduce the heat to low and, while whisking, slowly pour the milk and cornflour mixture into the simmering milk. Add the mastic and mix with a wooden spoon until the mixture thickens to a custard-like consistency, stirring continuously so it does not catch on the bottom. This will take 10–12 minutes.

Remove the saucepan from the heat and add the rosewater, stirring to combine. Allow the mixture to cool in the saucepan.

If using an ice-cream machine, follow the manufacturer's instructions. If not using an ice-cream machine, pour the mixture into a baking tin lined with plastic wrap and put it into the freezer. Every 30 minutes, run a fork through the mixture. This will need to be done 3–4 times, or until the ice cream is firm. This method will give you an icier version rather than the smoother one made in a machine.

If you cannot source good-quality pomegranate juice (which is available from delicatessens and some supermarkets) you can juice fresh pomegranates (see page 194). Each pomegranate will give you about 100 ml (3½ fl oz) of juice. If you have any pomegranates left over, you can make pomegranate mojitos (see page 194).

POMEGRANATE MOLASSES

MAKES ABOUT 500 ML (17 FL OZ/2 CUPS)

1 litre (35 fl oz/4 cups) good-quality
    or fresh pomegranate juice
200 g (7 oz) caster (superfine) sugar
100 ml (3½ fl oz) lemon juice

Put the pomegranate juice, sugar and lemon juice in a medium saucepan over medium–low heat and bring to a simmer. Reduce the heat to low and continue to simmer until the mixture is reduced to a thick syrup; this will take 20–30 minutes. Do not over-reduce the syrup as it may burn and become bitter. To judge the thickness, put a teaspoon in the freezer for 5 minutes and then dip it into the syrup, which will indicate how thick and reduced the molasses will be once it cools down. If it is not thick enough, cook it for several more minutes.

Transfer the molasses into a sterilised jar and store for up to 3 months in a cool, dark place. Refrigerate once opened.

A beautiful filling and topping for any number of dessert dishes, this saffron crème pâtissière is also recommended for breakfast with Evan's date & buttermilk pancakes with pistachio praline (see page 32). It is best made the day before you want to serve it.

SAFFRON CRÈME PÂTISSIÈRE

SERVES 4

pinch of saffron threads
500 ml (17 fl oz/2 cups) milk
125 g (4½ oz) caster
    (superfine) sugar
½ vanilla bean, halved lengthways
    and seeds scraped (optional)
4 large eggs, separated
zest of ½ lemon
30 g (1 oz) plain (all-purpose)
    flour, sifted
30 g (1 oz/¼ cup) cornflour
    (cornstarch), sifted

Soak the saffron in 1 tablespoon hot water and set aside.

Line a medium bowl with plastic wrap, leaving some excess to hang over the bowl (enough to fold back over, later in the recipe).

Combine the milk and saffron with its soaking water in a medium saucepan. Add 60 g (2¼ oz) of the sugar and the vanilla bean and seeds, if using. Place over medium–low heat and bring to a simmer.

Meanwhile, separate the eggs (reserving the 4 egg whites for the buttermilk pancakes, if desired). In a large bowl, whisk the egg yolks with the remaining sugar, the lemon zest, plain flour and cornflour until pale and thick.

Strain a little of the hot milk mixture through a sieve into the egg yolk mixture, whisking constantly. Continue straining in the milk mixture gradually and whisking.

Pour the mixture back into the saucepan. Place over medium heat and bring to a simmer, whisking continuously until the crème pâtissière becomes a smooth and glossy cream. Pour into the lined bowl. Fold the plastic wrap over, carefully pressing it onto the hot cream. (Be careful, it will be hot!) Transfer to the fridge and allow to chill until completely cool, about 2 hours.

Store the crème pâtissière in the fridge for up to 1 week.

This basic syrup keeps for up to a month in the fridge and can be used for cocktails, mocktails, coffee and iced tea. At Kepos Street Kitchen we use a raw (demerara) sugar syrup because the sugarcane molasses gives a beautiful flavour, but you can use any type of sugar.

RAW SUGAR SYRUP

MAKES 750 ML (26 FL OZ/3 CUPS)

500 g (1 lb 2 oz) raw (demerara) sugar
500 ml (17 fl oz/2 cups) boiling water

Put the sugar in a large jug. Pour the freshly boiled water over it and stir until the sugar has dissolved. Leave the syrup to cool, then pour into a bottle that holds 1 litre (35 fl oz/4 cups) and store in the fridge for up to 1 month.

Mum used to make her own yoghurt but didn't use a thermometer– it was all done by eye. And of course we kids always wanted the bought version. Now I appreciate how wonderful it was and I want to share it with you. Add any flavourings you like – vanilla bean and icing (confectioners') sugar or fresh fruit – or serve it with cakes.

HOMEMADE YOGHURT

MAKES ABOUT 1 KG (2 LB 4 OZ)

1 litre (35 fl oz/4 cups) full-cream (whole) milk
2 tablespoons active yoghurt (look for the words 'active culture' on the packaging)

Heat the milk in a saucepan to 75°C (170°F). Set aside for 30 minutes.

Add the active yoghurt and stir well with a wooden spoon. Pour into a sterilised 1 litre (35 fl oz/4 cup) jar or 4 x 250 ml (9 fl oz/1 cup) jars and seal well.

Fill a small esky (cooler box) with hot water. Put the jar(s) in it and leave for a minimum of 6 hours or overnight to make the yoghurt. Transfer the yoghurt to the fridge where it will keep for up to 5 days.

A basic tahini dressing is great to serve with fish, use as a dip, dollop over hummus or even use as a salad dressing. Make it thicker or thinner by using more or less tahini.

TAHINI DRESSING

MAKES ABOUT 500 ML (17 FL OZ/2 CUPS)

2 garlic cloves, peeled
1 tablespoon sea salt flakes
280 g (10 oz) tahini

Put the garlic, salt and 200 ml (7 fl oz) water in a food processor or blender and blend to a paste. Add the tahini and blend until combined. Transfer to a sterilised jar and store in the fridge for up to 7 days.

Gremolata is best made using a mortar and pestle. This one has lots of uses but is particularly delicious with the osso buco with jerusalem artichokes (see page 140).

CORIANDER GREMOLATA

MAKES ABOUT 600 G (1 LB 5 OZ)

4 garlic cloves, peeled
1 large handful coriander (cilantro), roughly chopped
zest of 1 lemon
3 tablespoons good-quality extra virgin olive oil

Using a mortar and pestle, pound the garlic and salt until combined. Add the coriander and pound until almost a paste. Add the lemon zest and olive oil and stir to combine.

Containing both rice and noodles, this dish is great for kids. Serve it as a side with stews or slow-cooked dishes to add an additional texture to the meal.

VERMICELLI RICE

SERVES 6-8 AS A SIDE DISH

100 ml (3½ fl oz) light olive oil
80 g (2¾ oz) vermicelli noodles, broken into large pieces
200 g (7 oz/1 cup) white long-grain rice
375 ml (13 fl oz/1½ cups) water, just boiled

Heat 2 tablespoons of the olive oil in a medium frying pan over medium heat. Add the vermicelli noodles and cook for 3–4 minutes, until a light colour. Set aside.

Heat the remaining olive oil in a medium saucepan over medium–high heat for 1–2 minutes. Add the rice, stir to coat and cook for 1 minute. Add the water and bring to the boil. Cover the saucepan with a tight-fitting lid, turn the heat to low and cook for 20 minutes. Remove from the heat and allow the rice to sit, lid on, for 5 minutes.

Remove the lid and fluff up the rice with a fork. Add the vermicelli noodles and gently stir through.

L–R: (STANDING) EVAN MURPHY, MICHAEL CVETKOSKI, ROY CHASON, MICHAEL RANTISSI; (SEATED) DOR HAREL, EVERTON MARTINS, SUJAN SHRESTHA.

Master these simple cooking techniques for the perfect result, every time.

HOW TO **COOK COUSCOUS**

SERVES 4

190 g (6¾ oz/1 cup) couscous
2–3 tablespoons olive oil
310 ml (10¾ fl oz/1¼ cups) boiling
    water or stock

Put the couscous in a stainless steel bowl and drizzle the oil over it. Gently rub the grains with your fingertips so they are coated with the oil, which will help give you a fluffier, less gluggy couscous.

Add the boiling water, season to taste with salt and stir to combine. Tightly cover the bowl with plastic wrap and allow the couscous to steam for 10–15 minutes.

When the couscous has absorbed the water, fluff it up with a fork and serve.

NOTE
For a savoury couscous, add a teaspoon of seasoning, such as ground turmeric, cumin or coriander, when you are rubbing the couscous with the oil. For a sweeter version, add a dash of vanilla sugar, or a pinch of ground cinnamon or freshly grated nutmeg, after the couscous has cooled and been fluffed.

HOW TO **COOK POLENTA**

MAKES A 20 CM X 20 CM (8 INCH X 8 INCH) TRAY

800 ml (28 fl oz) full-cream (whole) milk
20 g (¾ oz) butter
1 teaspoon sea salt flakes
200 g (7 oz) instant polenta

Line a 20 cm (8 inch) square baking tin with baking paper.

Put the milk, butter and salt in a medium saucepan over medium–high heat and bring to the boil. Once boiling, whisk in the polenta slowly until the mixture binds together. Change to a wooden spoon and stir until the polenta becomes firm but not too hard.

Spread the polenta evenly into the lined tin. Allow to cool in the fridge for at least 3 hours.

When ready to grill or pan-fry, turn the polenta out onto a chopping board, remove the baking paper and cut to the desired size and shape.

HOW TO COOK RICE

SERVES 4 AS A SIDE DISH

olive oil, for coating
200 g (7 oz/1 cup) basmati rice
375 ml (13 fl oz/1½ cups) boiling
water or stock

Place a saucepan with a lid over medium heat. Add enough olive oil to coat the bottom of the saucepan. Add the rice and stir to coat with the oil. Cook until the grains are toasted then add the water or stock. Add salt to taste and bring to the boil. Once boiling, put the lid on the saucepan and turn the heat down to the lowest setting. Cook with the lid on for 18 minutes.

Remove the saucepan from the heat and allow to rest for 5 minutes, keeping the lid on.

Remove the lid, fluff the grains with a fork and serve.

NOTE
The rice can be flavoured by adding 1 teaspoon of ground turmeric or a pinch of saffron threads when toasting it. Or add a kaffir lime leaf or a chunk of ginger when the water or stock has been added.

HOW TO STERILISE JARS & BOTTLES

To sterilise jars and bottles for storing jams, chutneys or mayonnaise, preheat the oven to 150°C (300°F). Wash the glassware in warm soapy water, rinse and put it in the oven for 15–20 minutes, until completely dry. Place the lids in a saucepan of boiling water and boil for 10 minutes. Remove with tongs and leave to dry on a clean tea towel (dish towel).

BUILDING YOUR PANTRY

The spices, herbs, seeds, grains and pulses that follow, as well as the kitchen fundamentals in the previous pages, are the building blocks I recommend for enjoying this style of cooking and eating. Most of the spices, blends and other ingredients will be available at the local supermarket, but if there is a Middle Eastern grocery store nearby, all the better. In terms of equipment, a sharp knife and chopping board, a basic set of pots and pans, serving plates and bowls, and a working stove and oven should pretty much do it.

SPICES

It is worth investigating whether there is a Middle Eastern or Mediterranean grocery store in your area so you can buy all of the ingredients you need in the one place. With spices, I like to buy the whole seeds and then toast and grind them as required, as toasting brings out the flavour of the spices and makes them more fragrant. Most are best stored in an airtight container in a cool, dark cupboard, and will last several months if kept this way.

ALLSPICE BERRY

A berry from an evergreen tree, allspice is picked and dried before it ripens. According to Jane Lawson's *Spice Market*, 'Allspice is considered Mother Nature's spice mix in a single berry'. If you can't find allspice, a good substitute is equal parts of cinnamon and mace, then half parts of cloves and pepper.
USES: Allspice is used a lot in savoury Middle Eastern dishes with rice and minced (ground) meat.

BAHARAT

A mixture that varies from region to region but will often include cinnamon or cassia bark, cumin, cardamom, nutmeg and cloves. The word 'baharat' means 'spice' in Arabic.
USES: As a dry rub for meats.

CARAWAY SEED

Also known as Persian cumin, the seeds come from the split halves of the dried fruit, and have aniseed notes, and warm and aromatic flavours. Dry-roasting before use brings out the oils and the flavours. It can be used whole or ground.
USES: Good for flavouring breads, casseroles, desserts and liqueurs.

CARDAMOM

The green and black/brown cardamom are separate species of the ginger family. In Arab countries cardamom is mainly used as a flavouring for coffee and the seeds are chewed to freshen breath.
USES: Green cardamom is mostly used for

flavouring desserts and teas, and black/brown cardamom – which is coarser in taste – is used more in meat and vegetable dishes. The ground seeds rather than the whole pods are traditionally chewed.

CASSIA

Resembling cinnamon and sold similarly in sticks (quills) and in powdered form, cassia is reddish-brown in colour and has a much more robust flavour than cinnamon.
USES: Use as for cinnamon but expect a robust rather than delicate flavour.

CINNAMON

A common and ever-popular spice, cinnamon comes from an evergreen tree related to the laurel or bay leaf family. It comes in stick (quill) and powdered forms.
USES: Cinnamon is used in Middle Eastern tagines and other slow-cooked dishes.

CHILLIES

There are more than 300 varieties of chilli from five main species.
USES: For an extra kick in Middle Eastern cooking.

CORIANDER SEED

Coriander seed is the dried ripe fruit of the plant that gives us the fresh herb. It is available in seed and powdered form, and has been used as a spice since ancient times.
USES: It is mainly used in savoury cooking but also works well with apples and can be used in cakes.

CUMIN SEED

The cumin plant is a member of the parsley family, and its dried ripe seeds – which can be dry-roasted whole or ground to a powder – have an earthy and slightly bitter flavour.
USES: Mainly used in Mediterranean cooking but with many applications in Middle Eastern dishes.

FENNEL SEED

Wild fennel is used for seeds (the other two varieties are for fennel used as a vegetable). Arab spice traders took this seed from the Mediterranean to the Middle East, then later to East Asia and India. If fennel and dill are grown near each other they will cross-fertilise.
USES: Used in spice mixes, tagines, bastilla and fish dishes, and also in desserts.

FENUGREEK

The spice is the dried ripe fruit of the fenugreek plant, which is a member of the pea and clover family. Its aroma resembles celery, and when roasted it smells like burnt sugar or maple. It needs slow-roasting to bring out its flavour fully but overheating makes the seeds taste bitter.
USES: Often used in spice blends, curries and oils, and can be used in desserts.

MASTIC

The sap or resin from the mastic (also known as the lentisk) tree or shrub. It comes in hard crystalline lumps and is often crushed before use.
USES: Often paired with rosewater and used to make Turkish delight, as well as desserts, breads, ice cream and puddings, and to add flavour to stews.

NUTMEG

Along with mace, this spice comes from the nutmeg tree and is available whole or powdered.
USES: Used with meat, rice and desserts, and mixed with sugar. It's best to use it freshly grated.

CUMIN SEEDS

WHOLE NUTMEG

CRUSHED CHILLI

GROUND CUMIN

FENUGREEK

GROUND TURMERIC

GROUND NUTMEG

GROUND CINNAMON

SESAME SEEDS

CARAWAY SEEDS

CORIANDER SEEDS

GROUND CORIANDER

PAPRIKA

ZA'ATAR

STAR ANISE

CINNAMON STICKS

CARDAMOM PODS

SAFFRON

SUMAC

BAHARAT

PAPRIKA

The familiar pungent red spice is the dried ground fruit of *Capsicum annuum*, the mild capsicum fruit often called pimento. It exists in many varieties, some of them very hot. 'Regular' paprika is normally mild and sweet and can be used generously. Smoked paprika gets its distinctive smoky flavour from a slow drying process over oak-burning fires.
USES: Mostly used in stews, when it is often mixed with flour, but also good with many meats and fish, and in marinades and dressings.

SAFFRON

Prized since the dawn of civilisation, saffron is the dried stigma of a flower from the crocus family. It is quite expensive due to the complex harvesting process involved.
USES: Used in rice dishes, tagines and stews, and in dressings and desserts. You only need a small amount when cooking. In *The Spice Book*, Arabella Boxer explains how to maximise the flavour of saffron: gently toast it over low heat, then crush using a mortar and pestle, add a couple of spoonfuls of hot liquid such as stock or water and leave to infuse for 5 minutes.

SESAME SEEDS

Reportedly one of the oldest seeds consumed by humans according to Jane Lawson's *Spice Market*, which also reveals an interesting fact: 'Plants are harvested prior to being fully ripe, as when ripe they spontaneously shatter. This act of nature is said to be the basis of the phrase "open sesame" from *The Arabian Nights*.' Sesame seeds are very nutritious but also high in kilojoules/calories because they comprise about 50 per cent oil.
USES: Sesame seeds are ground to make tahini and used in spice blends (for example dukkah), falafel, desserts or as a garnish in Middle Eastern cooking. They are used quite differently in Asian cuisine.

STAR ANISE

Woody and aniseed in flavour, and beautiful to look at, star anise comes from an evergreen tree related to the magnolia family. Its shape is an eight-pointed star, and it is said to be 13 times sweeter than sugar.
USES: Used in teas, marinades, spice blends, stews and desserts.

SUMAC

Sumac is the dried fruit of a shrub related to the cashew tree. It is ground into a powder that is sour and tart in flavour. It was originally a source of citrus flavour for the Egyptians in their cooking. Packaged sumac may contain salt to help preserve its flavour.
USES: Features in za'atar and is used in marinades and dressings, in breads and as a garnish.

TURMERIC

A member of the ginger family, this brightly coloured spice is also known as 'poor man's saffron'. Turmeric imparts an earthy flavour, is a natural antiseptic and is good to use for preserving. Best purchased in its ground form.
USES: Used in chermoula, and to add an earthy flavour to savoury dishes.

VANILLA

The vanilla pod is the fruit of a climbing orchid from Central America. It is the second most expensive spice in the world after saffron – expensive because of the processes involved in turning the pod to a bean. You can make your own vanilla essence by splitting a vanilla bean and soaking it in pure alcohol, such as vodka, for 2–3 weeks.
USES: Great in sweet dishes.

GRAINS & PULSES

I like to buy my supplies from Middle Eastern grocery stores as I know they will have all that I need and the turnover of their products will be high. Transfer your bags of grains and pulses to airtight containers as soon as you get them home, and store them in a cool, dark place.

BARLEY

This member of the grass family is one of the earliest cultivated plants. Pearl barley is the most common.
USES: Mostly used in soups and salads but can also be used for desserts.

BURGHUL

Its name is the Persian word for 'bruised grain', and it is also known as bulgur wheat. It has a light, nutty flavour and is actually wheat that has been cooked, had its bran removed, dried and then ground into grains.
USES: Burghul is one of the main ingredients in tabouleh and kibbeh.

CHICKPEAS

A type of pod, with each containing 2–3 peas, this small legume dates back to 800 BC. There are three types of chickpeas but the kabuli variety is mainly used in Middle Eastern and Mediterranean cooking. Chickpeas are high in protein and an important food in many parts of the world. Dried chickpeas need soaking prior to cooking but the tinned form are cooked. There is also chickpea flour, or besan.
USES: The main ingredient in hummus, chickpeas are also used in salads and tagines, and can be roasted and eaten as a snack.

COUSCOUS

Traditionally made from freshly ground whole grain, but not a 'grain' as such, couscous is made of tiny little balls of dough. It can be started with a bowl of semolina flour sprinkled with salted water. Fingers are then rubbed through the flour in a sweeping round motion, which causes the dough to form tiny balls. The balls are then dried, steamed and separated again to create the 'grains'. There are various kinds, including popular pre-cooked 'instant' couscous, and the larger-grained 'giant' couscous varieties, such as pearl, Israeli and moghrabieh.
USES: Used in both savoury or sweet dishes.

FREEKEH

A roasted green wheat where the young green stalks are harvested, gathered in bunches, then roasted and cracked. Freekeh is commonly referred to as an ancient grain, and it is thought to date back to around 2300 BC, when a town in the Eastern Mediterranean came under siege. To prevent imminent starvation, the townsfolk harvested their crops early and stored the green wheat, but the stockpiles caught on fire and the outer grains were burnt. However, they found that rubbing the burnt wheat heads together revealed the toasted grains inside, and they called this freekeh, which means 'the rubbed one'. It's very popular in Middle Eastern and North African cuisines.
USES: Used in salads and soups.

LENTILS

Growing in pods that contain 1–2 seeds on a small bushy plant, lentils are the best-known members of the legume family. There are numerous kinds, varying in size, colour, flavour and length of cooking time necessary, including red, green and brown, and the small French, or puy, lentil. They are low in fat, and high in protein and fibre, and an important food source in many cultures.
USES: Used in soups, salads, stews and patties.

SPLIT DRIED BROAD BEANS

A nutty flavoured bean when dried and split.
USES: Roasted as a snack or used to make falafel, dips, stews, curries and soups.

COUSCOUS

BARLEY

SPLIT DRIED
BROAD BEANS

MOGHRABIEH

FREEKEH

CHICKPEAS

BROWN LENTILS

RED LENTILS

BURGHUL

ISRAELI COUSCOUS

KAILI VAARD (LEFT) AND NICOLE BASNAKOVA.

ACKNOWLEDGEMENTS

Writing this cookbook has been an amazing experience and there are many people to thank.

First of all Jill Dupleix and Terry Durack, for believing in us and the food we serve at Kepos Street Kitchen. It has been an extraordinary opportunity to work with you both. You are the fairy godparents of this beautiful cookbook and we can't thank you enough for putting the idea forward to Murdoch Books and your mentoring throughout the process.

Thank you to all the amazing people at Murdoch Books. Sue Hines for your initial confidence in us, and your guidance and enthusiasm. Corinne Roberts for being so supportive and encouraging, and understanding about our other commitments during this project. You were the voice of calm and reason throughout, and no one could have asked for a better publisher. Virginia Birch for keeping us on track and giving us the freedom to express ourselves, but reining us in when necessary – our random suggestions for the photo shoots come to mind. Vivien Valk for co-ordinating the photo shoots and for the changing of locations to accommodate our crazy schedules, all with ease. Sarah Odgers, your vision and design for this book is so beautiful and we fell in love with the first draft pages even before we saw the proofs. We feel you have perfectly matched your design to our personalities. Lucy Tumanow-West for your infinite patience with us.

The many late-night and early-morning emails back and forth were certainly worth it and we are very proud of the end product. Thanks to everyone for your words of encouragement throughout this project.

Alan Benson and Jane Hann, thank you for the outstanding photography and beautiful styling. Alan, what an incredible photographer you are – so professional, calm and relaxed, but all with such good humour – and how fortunate we were to have worked with you. Jane, your eye for detail and your amazing styling ability made the food look happy and the shots come alive. Thank you for making the food the hero. We loved working with you both.

Thank you to the Frawley family for embracing this cuisine and welcoming my heritage to the fold. To Diane and Peter Frawley for letting us take over your home for the first few days of the shoot, and being so accommodating and supportive. And for being so proud of us.

Jana Frawley, thank you for your professional guidance and assistance, and your beautiful words.

Thank you to the McLeod family for enduring Monday evening after Monday evening at our house during the recipe-testing phase. We hope having to taste all that food wasn't too hard ... Thanks also to all the recipe testers. Caroline McLeod, we hope you can perfect the hummus recipe.

Serge Dansereau, thanks for the lovely words in your foreword. Without The Bathers' Pavilion none of this would be possible.

Thank you to all the wonderful staff at Kepos Street Kitchen – Kaili Vaard, Michael Cvetkoski, Nicole Basnakova, Roy and Shiri Chason, Evan Murphy, Christian Rosenmai, Sujan Shrestha, Everton Martins, Emil Heitz and Sada Fletcher – and all past staff and those to come. This book is as much a celebration of modern Middle Eastern food as it is about Kepos Street Kitchen. We've had a pretty extraordinary few years and we couldn't have done it without your loyal and unwavering support. A special thank you to Ladislav Smid, our very talented and creative Bar Manager, who worked closely with us to create the Drinks & Teas chapter in this book.

I would love to say a special thanks to a very special person – Kristy Frawley, my life partner. You have been incredible making sense of all those bits of scrap paper with the illegible scribble that I called recipes. Thank you for believing in me and my vision. Even in the hardest moments, when I had just $20 in my bank account, you made me believe it could still be done. Thanks for all the hard work, inspiration and motivation, all the sleepless nights and long hours.

INDEX

Published in 2015 by Murdoch Books, an imprint of Allen & Unwin
Reprinted twice 2016

Murdoch Books Australia
83 Alexander Street
Crows Nest NSW 2065
Phone: +61 (0) 2 8425 0100
Fax: +61 (0) 2 9906 2218
murdochbooks.com.au
info@murdochbooks.com.au

Murdoch Books UK
Ormond House
26–27 Boswell Street
London WC1N 3JZ
Phone: +44 (0) 20 8785 5995
murdochbooks.co.uk
info@murdochbooks.co.uk

For Corporate Orders & Custom Publishing, contact our Business Development Team
at salesenquiries@murdochbooks.com.au.

Publisher: Corinne Roberts
Editorial Manager: Virginia Birch
Design Manager: Vivien Valk
Designer: Sarah Odgers
Editor: Lucy Tumanow-West
Photographer: Alan Benson
Stylist: Jane Hann
Production Manager: Mary Bjelobrk, Rachel Walsh

Text © Michael Rantissi and Kristy Frawley 2015
The moral rights of the authors have been asserted.
Design © Murdoch Books 2015
Photography © Alan Benson 2015

A cataloguing-in-publication entry is available from the catalogue of the National Library
of Australia at nla.gov.au.

ISBN 978 1 74336 467 3 Australia
ISBN 978 1 74336 444 4 UK

A catalogue record for this book is available from the British Library.

Colour reproduction by Splitting Image Colour Studio Pty Ltd, Clayton, Victoria
Printed by C & C Offset Printing Co. Ltd., China

IMPORTANT: Those who might be at risk from the effects of salmonella poisoning (the elderly,
pregnant women, young children and those suffering from immune deficiency diseases) should
consult their doctor with any concerns about eating raw eggs.

OVEN GUIDE: You may find cooking times vary depending on the oven you are using.
For fan-forced ovens, as a general rule, set the oven temperature to 20°C (35°F) lower
than indicated in the recipe.

MEASURES GUIDE: We have used 20 ml (4 teaspoon) tablespoon measures. If you are using a 15 ml
(3 teaspoon) tablespoon, add an extra teaspoon of the ingredient for each tablespoon specified.

BIBLIOGRAPHY
Boxer, Arabella, *The Hamlyn Spice Book*, Hamlyn, UK, 1997.
Hospitality Magazine (hospitalitymagazine.com.au).
Lawson, Jane, *Spice Market*, Murdoch Books, Sydney, 2008.